To Kevin (K1):
Thank you for your
leadership and service!
Charl

Thinking Aloud

Thinking Aloud

—⚋—

Reflections on Ethical Leadership

Charles A. Weinstein Ph.D.
Ethical Leaders in Action LLC

Dedication

For Jacob, Edie, and Alex. So much *nachas*.
For Cathy, always.

Table of Contents

Introduction

Welcome!

T here are many books about leadership, ranging from brilliant to embarrassing. Thank you for choosing *Thinking Aloud*, a collection of essays intended to help you reflect and grow as an effective, ethical leader. The ideas on these pages arose from my experiences as a follower, as a leader, and as a consultant and teacher. In each of these contexts, I have been very fortunate to learn from others. This book is intended to share that learning with you.

I began writing essays on leadership and ethics in 2007, but my curiosity and interest in leadership began much earlier. Through high school and college, I held entry-level jobs as a laborer, in the retail sector, and in food service. One observation from these early experiences continues to inform my work today: my co-workers and I always worked harder and performed better when our supervisors helped us to understand and remember that our work mattered. I will never take meaningful work for granted, and will always appreciate and value work that is not just valuable, but interesting and engaging, as well. To a great extent, leaders can help others to find meaning and maintain a sense of purpose in their work. Maintaining and reinforcing a sense of purpose is a core function of leadership.

After graduating from college with a degree in philosophy, I followed the well-worn path from the study of humanities to work in information technology. The Personal Computer (PC) was less than 10 years old, Microsoft Windows was not fully developed, and many businesses were struggling to realize the productivity benefits they had sought through desktop computerization. Ironically, it was working with then-emerging technology that helped me realize the timeless power of human leadership in the workplace. More often than not, it was leadership, not technology, that ultimately drove – or inhibited – productivity.

In one instance, I worked as part of a team to automate a labor union claims process. Our work helped the client to reduce the process duration from three weeks to less than three days. Immediately, the new desktop computers were seen as the driver of productivity. The reality was different. As we began to talk with the people responsible for processing claims, it became apparent that these workers didn't know what their teammates were doing, or how their work fit into the broader claims process. Co-workers didn't communicate, and they didn't trust one another. By solving these problems first, we were able to reduce the claims process timeline from three weeks to four days. By automating that improved process, we further reduced the time to less than three days. The greatest power, then, was not in automation, but in coordinating efforts, and in assuring that teammates communicated and worked together effectively. These, too, are core functions of leadership.

I have worked for more than 25 years as a consultant and manager, serving the largest companies in the world and the newest, smallest start-ups. I have worked in industries ranging from education to medical devices and from consumer products to mining. Each of these contexts has its own language, and its own unique challenges. What they all have in common, however, is that human beings do the work. Consistently, we human beings do our best work, and find that work most rewarding, when we have effective leaders.

My perspective on leadership is also informed by my academic background: I trained to be an ethics professor, earned a Ph.D., and ultimately have sought to adapt and apply theoretical ethical concepts to the practical world of work. In 2007 I began to do that work full-time as the founding director of the Hill Center for Ethical Business Leadership, then a division of the James J. Hill Reference Library.

Since 2010 I have done so through my own firm, Ethical Leaders in Action (ethinact.com).

The public and private sectors have embraced ethics in one respect: compliance programs created in the wake of ethical lapses train people to avoid and mitigate a host of bad actions. Yet, as we will explore in these pages, that compliance-based conception of ethics fails to recognize the real power of ethics: not just to keep us from doing wrong, but to help us to do and be our best. My intent is to present a positive perspective on ethics, through approaches that are imaginative, relevant, and sometimes even entertaining. The view of ethics that I strive to apply is focused not merely on avoiding bad actions, but on being our best and leading meaningful lives, in constructive relationships with others. I call it, simply, "ethical leadership." Ethical leaders empower others to improve the world, in ways both large and small, globally and locally.

The learning process continues. Today, I spend my time with leaders in fire and police departments, nursing homes, professional service firms, manufacturers, and service companies. We work together to implement ethical leadership principles and practices. In the course of this work, I have observed that every leader I have come to admire has been committed to his or her own growth and development. Everyone has things to learn, and insights to share. The essays on following pages invite you to join us in learning and growing as leaders. We're all in this together, and we might as well share our stories, and a few laughs, along the way.

Thinking...Allowed

This book's singular goal is to encourage and stimulate you to think, and thereby to grow as a leader. You can do this alone, by selecting an essay or two at a time, or by reading the work as a whole. The selections also lend themselves to team discussions, allowing team members to respond to the essays and to one another, growing closer as a team in the process. Please take the ideas in this book, consider them as you see fit, and make of them what you will.

This book is intentionally modest in scope; this too is based on lessons learned from others. As young men, the philosophers David

Charles A. Weinstein Ph.D.

Hume and Ludwig Wittgenstein each set out to write major books, offering conclusive answers to giant questions. The resulting works were impressive: Hume's aptly named *Treatise of Human Nature (1740)* and Wittgenstein's *Tractatus Logico-Philosophicus (1921)*, which set out (roughly) to articulate the relationships between language, truth and science. These books are *performances*. Readers are struck by each author's intellectual prowess, his brilliance. We confront these authors' ideas.

When his *Treatise* flopped, critically and professionally, Hume refocused and revised his ideas, creating his most influential work, *An Inquiry Concerning Human Understanding* (1748), and a series of *Discourses* on related topics. Wittgenstein's later works are similarly entitled *Investigations*, and they replaced the assertion of answers with the exploration of questions. These works are *conversations*. Readers are invited to consider both challenges and assertions. We are rewarded by the opportunity to consider, to think, and to grow. Reading these works helps us to reveal, develop, and clarify our own ideas.[1]

Thinking Aloud seeks admission to this latter tradition, with less weight and more laughs than either Hume or Wittgenstein provided. For the past five years, I have worked with some remarkable leaders in corporate and health care workplaces that were already quite familiar to me. I've also worked in places I never thought I would be: the worlds of cops, firefighters and emergency medical service (EMS) responders.[2] I've learned a great deal about the practices, and the languages, of leadership. I've also learned how much I don't yet know about the varied arts of bringing out the best in people. I am committed to this journey of discovery, and grateful for the many wonderful leaders (and a few knuckleheads) whom I've met along the way.

---

[1] I am grateful to Professor Emeritus Douglas Lewis, my friend, teacher and mentor, for helping me clarify this relevant intellectual history of these two titanic thinkers.

[2] I use the term "cops" to refer to law enforcement professionals, across ranks and agency affiliations. I use it with respect, because that is the term that my clients and friends in law enforcement most often use to refer to themselves.

Organized Collections of Ideas

The essays collected in this book arise from my journey to cultivate, improve, and inspire ethical leaders in action, to date. These ideas emerged in specific moments in time; most of the essays have previously appeared as blog posts.[3] Therefore, I have included the month and year in which they were written. Some have also been revised or retitled to make them more relevant in the context of this book. The essays are organized into four collections, presented as sections or chapters:

I. *An Emerging Perspective* includes essays on the core ideas that animate Ethical Leadership as a set of commitments and practices. This includes a framing of corporate social responsibility as a strategic investment in business relationships.

II. *On Living Like a Grown-Up* reflects my ongoing challenge to act more like the balding, middle-aged man that others see. It takes some measure of reflection to act with maturity, fulfilling our responsibilities, while having some fun along the way.

III. *In the Public Square* considers the challenges of leadership in public life. These were among the first topics of philosophy, as when Socrates stopped strangers in the Athenian marketplace to ask questions that...ultimately led to his demise. (No thinkers were harmed in the writing of this book, however.)

IV. *In the Workplace: Relationships and Organizations* considers how we live and work together, or how we ought to do so. Ethics is about living a meaningful life, in relationships with others. Much of our work takes place, inherently, in and around teams and organizations. Essays in this section present practical applications of ethical leadership concepts at work.

I am skeptical of treatises, and of people who think they possess answers so large, or so numerous, as to fill them. I'm intrigued by inquiries. The following essays are intended to intrigue you, and invite you to reflect and to develop as an ethical leader. All of the opinions expressed in this book are my own. Of course, I hope that you find things here with which you agree, perhaps even resonate. By the same

[3] See the *ethinact* blog of Ethical Leaders in Action, LLC (www.ethinact.com) and the vibrant community blog, *Leadership and Community* (www.leadershipandcommunity.com), to which I am a grateful contributor.

token, you are free, even encouraged, to disagree. If the disagreement is interesting, the essay has done its job. As I like to tell clients, I reserve the right to be mistaken and to still be of value. If engaging and disagreeing with these ideas helps you to frame and strengthen your own perspective, then the inquiry was valuable.

Bring your Friends (or Teammates)

Many of these essays arise out of conversations, and one great way to use them is in conversation. We learn and grow together, as leaders and as persons of character. To facilitate discussions, I have included "Conversation Starters" after every essay. Use them to explore your own thoughts about leadership and life, especially in conversation with others.

You can also use this book as a team-building and development tool. Try this approach, or create your own:

1. Select a reading and discussion team leader, or set out a rotating schedule of leaders throughout a year.
2. Establish a regular meeting time, when team members can gather informally for as little as 15 minutes, or as long as you want.
3. Read one essay per week, or a few essays for less-frequent meetings. Let group members choose the essays, and the leader can pick from the Conversation Starters, or create new questions for discussion.

Invite your team members to read, to think, and to share their thoughts. Have some conversations, and see what works for you.

Part I

An Emerging Perspective

My primary philosophical interest has always been ethics: the study of morality – what is right and wrong, good and bad. Ethics helps us understand and apply morality to our lives. When it became clear to me that my natural habitat is business rather than a university, it was natural for me to focus my studies on business ethics.

Western society has made a hash of ethics as an enterprise. Scholars earn prestige by focusing on the most arcane features of highly theoretical works. Business ethicists who seek to apply theory overwhelmingly do so in order to define, and ultimately prevent, really bad behavior. When an act of genuine evil – or of garden-variety scumbaggery – makes the paper, people in my audiences often ask for my opinion of the act or the actor. Generally, my opinions on those matters aren't very interesting. Neither is the news itself, from an ethical perspective. Nearly all of us do wrong, in small ways, some of the time, and a few folks do great wrong much of the time. That's not good, which is why we call it, "wrong." Most of the time, those audience members want to hear me proclaim that a wrongdoer is a criminal or a greedy bastard. If that is the primary way we use applied ethics, why should anyone care much about it?

And yet, society invests in applied ethics, of a sort. Laws like the Sarbanes-Oxley Act and the Federal Sentencing Guidelines for Organizations (known as "SOX" and "FSGO," or as l prefer to think of these measures, "The Full Employment for Consultants Acts") make it foolish for companies to function without an ethics program that includes training. Elected and appointed officials likewise want the air cover provided by ethics programs for their public employees. Mostly, such training programs are designed to help people recognize what is morally wrong and/or against the rules, to avoid those actions, to report them, and to mitigate the harm – *or else.* No wonder people dread ethics training. Few people like to belabor the obvious. Nobody likes to be scolded in advance.

Ethics ought to be positive, and not simply negative. Rather than focusing on what we should not do, it can, and should, give us guidance on what we can do to be our best. I began to do this work because positive ethics has yet to realize its potential impact on the world of work. As I consult and teach, I learn so much about the worlds in which my clients and students work. In all instances, I learn from ethical leaders whose words and actions reflect the desire and commitment to be our best. These people empower others to improve the world, in ways large and small.

I also learn from the questions, and especially the challenges, posed by program participants. Skepticism is a beautiful thing. Seeking to teach audiences in general, and answering skeptics in particular, have led me to think and write about what have become a core set of ideas about ethical leadership. The following essays concern those ideas. Because these essays concern the theoretical foundations of my work, many of them arose from teaching activities. Others are focused on the workplace.

Spending Life

July 2009

We grilled and devoured this year's first sweet corn. We like to wait until it appears at the Saint Paul Farmer's Market – which means it was grown within 50 miles of here. *To everything there is a season*, and thus begins the season of sweet corn, here in the near-northern climes.

I am repeatedly stunned by the acceleration of the seasons through my adulthood. This is no novel observation; I have read explanations that our perception of time is relative to our age. A year constitutes 20 percent of the life of a 5-year-old, and (insert much smaller percentage here) of my life.[4] That causal explanation, while intuitively compelling, fails to capture the power of the phenomenon. We can feel its real power as a sense of urgency to pursue that which is important. How do we spend our lives?

Unlike our money, we have no choice but to spend our lives: we can't save our time for later. We can make choices that are likely to extend life, and we may face circumstances or make choices that shorten it. Except under dire circumstances, we can't know our remaining balance. But, regardless of their durations, we are forced

---

[4] This explanation is just one of many, but I won't pause to dive into that, um, timeless controversy. William James, for example, wrote beautifully on his view that time seems to fly faster as we age because when we are young, more things are novel.

to spend our lives. Happily, to a very great extent, we can determine how we do so.

Therein lays perhaps the most compelling argument for ethical conduct and the pursuit of greatness. In our work with clients and business students, ethical leadership consultants daily confront the question of why, in a competitive situation, one ought to go beyond legal compliance to act in accordance with one's moral sensibilities. Why should we do more than is required? Our discussions often address the long-term benefits of trust-based relationships and the nature of unexpected competitive advantage. I encourage business leaders to think creatively and act courageously in pursuit of outcomes that are both commercially and ethically great. It is not always the case that commerce and ethics align, but I believe that those outcomes are available more often than we might think, if we are willing and able to bring them about.

Perhaps the most basic reason to do so is at hand: because we have but one lifetime, we devote much of it to our work and we owe it to ourselves to spend that portion meaningfully. That includes doing work that matters, in ways that build relationships with others. It means taking the time to engage with others in meaningful pursuits, as well. This may mean going beyond a traditional conception of "acting ethically," to embrace a broader notion of acting honorably. In other words, let us use our precious time to do our best, and to be our best.

We should also enjoy the rewards of acting honorably: we can celebrate a job well done, a courageous or creative action, or an unexpected opportunity to help someone else. This celebration is a reward unto itself; it also reinforces our commitments. To enjoy a life well-lived is also to encourage the commitment to live well. A sense of duty can be compelling, but so can taking pleasure in doing the right thing, and some humble pride in acting honorably. Let us remember to enjoy some sweet corn along the way, as well.

—ɷ—

Conversation Starters:

One core concept of ethical leadership is simple, but not always easy to achieve: we ought to lead our lives mindfully, even honorably, and take some pleasure in doing so.

- What aspects of your life, at this point, are most satisfying for you?
- In what achievements, or commitments, do you take humble pride?
- What changes could you make now, to feel better about how you are spending your life three months, three years, or three decades from now?

Sisyphus on Parole: Finding Meaning in Our Work

October 2009

We can learn a great deal from the Greek myth of Sisyphus about finding joy and meaning in the daily grind.

You might recall (or rush to *Wikipedia* to discover) that Sisyphus committed some very impressive acts of hubris – culminating in freeing humanity from death (if only briefly) and revealing Zeus (king of the Olympian Gods) for the sexual scoundrel that he was.[5] Then Zeus exacted his revenge: Sisyphus was condemned to repeatedly push a boulder up a hill, reaching the top only to see the giant rock roll back down again. Zeus conceived a terrible sentence for an extremely clever and creative human: eternal, pointless labor.

Greek myths are not the only ancient source for this observation. The book of Exodus relates the tale of an angry Pharaoh punishing Israelite slaves with an act of caprice: ordering them to make the same quota of bricks with less straw to bind them. Older slaves were required to do the heavy lifting, while younger, stronger slaves were limited to lighter duty. Much more work, for the same amount of product. The

---

[5] In this way and others, the Greek gods were all too human. Not surprisingly, accounts of this story vary, but typically include Sisyphus talking Thanatos out of his original death sentence before a more creative sentence was imposed. By all accounts, Sisyphus was no dummy.

message: pointless labor is drudgery, demoralizing and dehumanizing. The emblem of meaningless work is toil that is unnecessarily arduous, and ultimately unproductive.

It is sometimes easy to feel the way Sisyphus and the Israelites felt about our own work: meet your quota this year, and the quota for next year is increased. The carrot recedes as we pursue it. If we followed ancient gender roles, Sisyphus would have *nothing* on Mrs. Sisyphus: clean the kitchen, cook the meal, repeat. Feed the baby, change the diaper....you get the picture. It is all too easy to let the rhythms of life become a dirge, the music by which we trudge through our days.

What's a mortal to do?

First, we can often choose to find meaning in our work and our tasks. We may have more control over the tasks themselves than we recognize. Even if we don't, we can look to their underlying goals – or to the achievements of our teams and organizations – for inspiration. We can also take justifiable pride in work well done and enjoy the benefits that we are creating for ourselves or others. We can seek to understand the value our customers seek and strive to improve on it. Striving is itself more satisfying than trudging. Preparing meals and cleaning the kitchen can be acts of love, repeated often (some weeks more often than others), and far from meaningless.

Caring about what we do, and taking justified pride in a job well done, can be transformative. This isn't mere misdirection, but a very real sort of magic: we change the nature of our work, by our insight and repeated acts of will. Meaningful work is fulfilling, satisfying, even ennobling. Even if you've never thought of it that way, I'll bet you've experienced it. I see it in myself, just as I see it in others. One day I take great pleasure in communicating with others, another day my teaching is a chore. One waiter really seems to enjoy serving people, exhibiting hospitality and participating in a satisfying meal. Another simply can't wait for his shift to end, and it shows. The irony: whose shift seems longer? We can't always feel like creative geniuses, but we can strive to do great work and take pride in the effort, as well as the achievement.

More important, we shouldn't have to work that magic alone. As friends, teammates, and leaders, we can come together to build meaning into our work, and to take pride in our accomplishments. If we want to work for an organization that we can feel proud of, we need to lead the way in building that sort of an organization. We can seek to know and understand how our work impacts others, and we can share that understanding with the people with whom we share our work.

Do the team members you lead know how their tasks fit into the broader projects, processes or products that they produce? Do they know how their work benefits customers, or contributes to the firm's success? Or, do you just insist that the rocks keep rolling? These are messages that need to be repeated: not quarterly or weekly, but constantly. You cannot over-communicate where making meaning is concerned.

By building a sense of meaning and purpose into the work that you share, you demonstrate respect for your team members as human beings. You also empower them to join you in the pursuit of greatness.

—m—

Conversation Starters:
Finding and maintaining a meaningful sense of purpose in our work is essential for maintaining our own productivity, as well as our quality of life. Helping others do so is a key function of effective leaders.

- Have you ever experienced a "Sisyphean crisis," where all of your work felt pointless and endless? What did you do to climb out of it?
- What can you do to help others who are stuck?
- How do you celebrate the purpose in your work?

Ode to Candor

March 2008

I am currently teaching an undergraduate business course, a unit for graduating seniors. In the course of that work, the students asked for some basic guidance. Before we could turn to more strategic matters of enterprise-wide social responsibility, they wanted to consider business ethics from a more personal perspective. We talked about bringing personal values and ethical perspectives to the workplace. We also discussed, in very practical and specific terms, how to talk about ethical issues with superiors, peers, and subordinates. The discussion left me with a renewed appreciation of the power and, sadly, the scarcity of candor in our business lives.

What do we really mean?

Candid communicators speak their minds. Effective leaders do so tactfully, to a degree appropriate to the situation. Honesty is necessary but not sufficient for true candor: an honest speaker may share all or part of what he believes to be true, while a candid speaker shares what she is thinking, what she believes to be true, and why. That's a high bar, requiring both self-awareness and a keen sense of the situation. It also requires courage, at times, to truly and accurately express thoughts and beliefs. The payoff can be equally high, though. Meetings achieve the best possible outcomes when knowledgeable people share openly.

Trust is established because – well, it's obvious, isn't it? We tend to trust people who are richly and fully honest with us.

Moreover, a lack of candor can be costly. Years ago, I found myself splitting a week between clients in San Diego and Stamford, Connecticut. Monday and Tuesday, we worked in San Diego, hearing nothing but vaguely positive feedback from that client. We then flew east, and spent the rest of the week being criticized, pointedly and at times profanely, by the second client, who was concerned about the emerging direction of our work. By Friday, my longing for Southern California went well beyond the weather.

However…the San Diego client terminated our work shortly after our sunny sessions, without ever explaining why. An expensive project was shelved at its midpoint. They never returned my calls, emails, and letters. Nobody won. In Connecticut, we changed direction based on the client's input and successfully completed the project. The products of our work were still in use years later. That level of candor wasn't comfortable, but it paid off for everyone involved.

Many barriers to communication

Communicating candidly and clearly can be difficult for many reasons. Often, we're afraid to say what is on our minds, for fear of exposing ourselves to criticism or ridicule. We may pull our punches to avoid embarrassing or offending our friends, or obscure our true beliefs to avoid arming our adversaries. Sometimes discretion is in order; determining the appropriate level of candor can be a delicate process in and of itself. Even when it is appropriate, candid communication requires courage and skill.

The manner of candid communication must be appropriate to the audience. Anthropologist Edward T. Hall and others have described a distinction between high-context and low-context cultures.[6] The distinction is rich and interesting, but for our purposes I will summarize as follows: low-context cultures rely primarily on the words that are spoken;

---

[6] Edward Twitchell Hall was a 20th-century anthropologist who developed the concept of high- and low-context cultures, which he explored in the book, *Beyond Culture* (1976). He is also widely acknowledged as a founder of intercultural communication as an academic field.

high-context cultures require that speakers and listeners understand a great deal more about the way in which those words are used, by whom, and under what circumstances.

The standard examples of high-context cultures include China, where often what is said in a meeting is less important than who says it, or even where people are seated at the table. I would argue that we need not travel so far to find high-context communication in action. Even in, say, South Dakota, the word "yes," spoken with a particular hesitation or head tilt, can mean "over my dead body." I'm told it's the same in Japan, where a sharp intake of breath means that the word "yes" actually communicates "no way." Candor is predicated on communicating appropriately for the context.

Candor is worth the effort

We can all play a role in overcoming challenges to clear communication. Speakers can be courageous about sharing what is truly on their minds, and both sensitive and knowledgeable enough to do so in ways which are understood by everyone involved and appropriate to the situation. Listeners likewise can engage all their senses, and interpret what they hear and see based on an enlightened understanding of context. How many times have you misconstrued an email because you couldn't see a twinkling eye or hear a playful tone of voice?

I learned the hard way in San Diego. In retrospect, it seems likely that I was the only one in the room who was anticipating our next meeting. Whether that misleading communication was a pure lack of candor, or whether the clients were candid but I missed the cues, will never be known. Considerable time and money were wasted as a result.

Establishing and maintaining an environment where people can communicate candidly and respectfully isn't always easy, but it is worth the effort. Much of the value of a truly diverse working team can be lost if participants cannot openly share ideas and perspectives. The effectiveness of communication across teams or companies can make or break deals. In every business context, the critical element of trust depends upon communication that is richly truthful and mutually clear.

—⟋⟍—

Conversation Starters:

Communicating with appropriate candor is a talent worth developing, and a commitment that is worth maintaining even when it is particularly difficult.

- When is candor particularly challenging for you?
- Can you recognize these challenges and rise to these occasions?
- When you did, how did it work out?

Embracing Complexity

November 2009

I sometimes teach ethics courses at the Carlson School of Management at the University of Minnesota. Those students always seem to come up with interesting perspectives and concerns that I otherwise would not have paused to consider. (Engaged students are pesky, but in a good way.) Last week, we considered whether and how to talk to employees about job security, especially when their jobs are less than secure. I went into the discussion with a firmly-held point of view, grounded in the idea that trust is both a primary ethical consideration and a powerful business driver. Nothing builds trust like reliable candor and transparency, so these should be the principles that guide our actions. As we talked it through, the students stressed other considerations, like the very real need to protect some key assets from some employees, and the likelihood that even a modest level of expressed risk would be taken with alarm. They noted the weaknesses of prediction. The discussion complicated my perspective, by broadening it. Other conversations have had similar effects.

The students generally stick with the discussion and embrace the complexity, but I can see that it's uncomfortable for some of them. That should come as no surprise: we business people are trained to revere simplicity, to reduce paragraphs to bullet points and conversations to elevator speeches. This can be a matter of discipline. Mark

Twain and others have observed that a good, short letter takes longer to write. We are taught to clarify, which often leads us to simplify. Clarity is good, so simple clarity is better, right?

Not always.

Misplaced simplicity can lead us past clarity and into emptiness. Some situations are complex, and to simplify their descriptions robs them of accuracy or meaning. Of course, we sometimes need the discipline to focus and simplify. Other times, we need the willingness to embrace complexity, and the skill to communicate about complicated things clearly, if not always briefly.

Yes, it's hard.

I recall one in-class discussion concerning the ethical status of social engagement. Starbucks touts its investment in environmental remediation. Do they do so because they care about the environment or because they want to sell more coffee? Does a company's desire to benefit commercially from good works taint those works? Do results count, or do motives matter more when we are making moral judgments that guide our commercial behavior (even at the latte level)?

To delve into these questions, it helps to tolerate complexity: we can say that our actions are driven by social AND commercial motives, and mean it. Why can't we act from both motives, truly and honestly, at the same time? Perhaps we could do well to accept that our most important questions often have more than one right answer, and that best answers may be inherently complicated.

—⚡—

Conversation Starters:
Do not fear complexity. Seek to clarify, and simplify only when you can do so without loss of meaning.
- What is the difference between brevity and clarity?
- Why do you think that business culture, in particular, has developed such a reverence for simplicity?
- How do you know whether you've simplified things enough, but not too much?

Actions and Words: Loud and Clear

October 2013

It is often said: "actions speak louder than words." It is one thing to support an effort with words, and another to contribute our time, our energies, or our resources. A sincere apology can constitute very important words, helping to heal and strengthen relationships after we do harm. But if that apology isn't supported by action, then words are not enough. Actions have spoken loudly.

On the other hand "loud" isn't always "clear." How often are actions alone misunderstood? How often does someone take the wrong action because we have not shared critical information like our needs, our wishes, or our intent? Actions without words can be risky, even reckless.

The truth is, we need both actions and words, especially as we work together on teams. We need words to guide and explain our actions, and we need actions to make good on our commitments and to realize our intentions. I am sure that none of this is surprising. Why, then, do some teammates so easily misunderstand one another?

Often, I think, our misunderstandings arise because we don't take the time to connect with one another, to discuss what actions ought to be taken, and to agree upon who will do what, when, and how. I have been working with one leadership team and much discussion has centered on its members' tendency to misunderstand, and ultimately mistrust, one another. They describe a deep frustration that has been building over the course of several years. At the heart of it, I think, is a pattern of misunderstanding actions and their underlying intent, in the absence of adequate conversation.

There's evidence to support this explanation. Participants note how often they leave a meeting with widely varied conclusions about what had been decided. Everyone may take action – in different directions. Each one of them remembers being angry with someone because of something he or she did, and not addressing it because they believed that the person in question "had to know what he was doing and that it was wrong." Often, of course, that was not the case. No wonder they are resentful.

The solution may be simple, if not easy. What would happen if we took the time to be explicit about the decisions we make together and the commitments we exchange? If we addressed problems as they occur? If, when we were not able to honor a commitment we made, we notified the affected parties as soon as possible, revised our commitments, and took it upon ourselves to mitigate any harm we caused? It is easy to imagine how much, and how quickly, teamwork could improve.

—〰—

Conversation Starters:
Let us take the time to thoughtfully align our words and actions.
- Can you think of a time when you misinterpreted someone else's actions? An instance when your actions were misinterpreted?
- What happened, and how might it have been avoided?
- When working on a team, do you pause to make sure that everyone is "on the same page?"

From Obligation to Opportunity

June 2008

As a business ethicist, I grew up repeatedly confronted by Milton Friedman's quote from a *New York Times Magazine* article: "*there is one and only one social responsibility of business — to use its resources and engage in activities designed to increase its profits so long as it stays within the rules of the game...*". The article was published on September 16, 1970, and almost continuously since then, writers in business ethics have used that single article as an argument from which to diverge. I'm so tired of it that I could barf. I hereby apologize for every time I have cited the article, including right now.

Almost 40 years ago, Friedman was responding to advocates for a broadly expanded view of managers' moral duties and obligations. By so doing, he made it all too easy for four decades' worth of lazy writers (including me) to jump into our own arguments for what managers ought to do, in contrast to Friedman's assertion that they simply ought to make money for shareholders.

What probably angered Milton Friedman in 1970, and continues to offend many managers today, was not so much the content of the message of social responsibility, but the tone of that message – too often couched in shrill, moralistic, finger-pointing invective. Nobody likes to be called scuzzy, and nobody likes to be told what to do. Almost everybody, by contrast, likes to be recognized as a leader and to be rewarded for wise investments. So why not think about social responsibility in more positive terms?

Managers do have a fiduciary responsibility to shareholders. They also have fundamental ethical responsibilities to the people who are touched by their businesses. Rather than argue solely about the nature of these duties – about the obligations that stakeholders impose on managers – we would do better, and go farther, by focusing instead on stakeholder relationships as strategic investment opportunities. By investing wisely in these relationships, managers can act in socially responsible ways while fulfilling their duty to shareholders. Their businesses will prosper by their wise investments.

By moving beyond the ethics of obligation to the ethics of opportunity, we open up a new realm for discussion among business leaders who are already inclined to do the right thing, just as they are motivated and driven by a desire to prosper. We still need to think about compliance with relevant laws, regulations and ethical norms. We ought not limit our thinking to those obligations, but continue thinking creatively about ways to win by going beyond them.

Aligning commercial success and social responsibility is an essentially creative undertaking. By looking at our businesses through this lens, we might create competitive advantage in the supply chain, by transforming transactional vendor agreements into shared destiny and mutually beneficial partnerships. We can create organizations that attract the best employees, and environments in which those people get even better over time. We connect with customers based on a commitment to truly serve them and an awareness of the benefits that excellence can confer on our own firms.

None of these benefits can accrue merely by following the rules. Compliance with ethical norms is a minimum – and failure to comply can undo much of the good we are seeking through our positive actions – but ethics is about more than compliance. Ethics is about living well and doing good. As one friend observed, "complying with ethical norms is like building a home in accordance with the building codes – that's just the minimum. Saying a house is built to code doesn't prove that it's a great house, just a minimally acceptable house." The real opportunities happen when we look for ways to build great things that others value.

As people concerned with ethical leadership, we need to minimize finger-wagging and moralizing, and maximize creative thinking and, for that matter, inspirational storytelling. By so doing, we help create more great stories to tell.

—⟋⟍—

Conversation Starters:

We ought to do more than avoid wrongdoing, and rejecting our worst possible actions. We will do better, in all respects, by considering our best options and acting in ways that are not just acceptable, but honorable.

- What stories can you tell about business or organizational leaders who go the extra mile to honor relationships?
- Do you look for these positive stories and share them?
- What examples from your own experience illustrate the ethics of opportunity?

Tough Times: The Best Time to Take the High Road

February 2009

I have some painful memories associated with a talk I gave in early 2009 to an undergraduate architecture and construction management class. We talked about ethical leadership, and I presented a set of techniques for avoiding conflicts and working through the inevitable conflicts that arise. One of the construction management students asked whether, in these tough economic times, people can really afford to think about ethics beyond what is minimally required.

Construction management students are a pragmatic bunch. Social responsibility without a well-defined return on investment (ROI) is a tough sell with them. I wanted desperately to make the case for that ROI because – as noted in the preceding essay – good business leaders can realize commercial benefit from a commitment to social responsibility, understood as a commitment to building strong, trust-based relationships.

Sadly, I muffed it. His was a classic question, whether doing the right thing makes business sense. I answered it with a ramble of (accurate) statements and (true) observations, instead of a clear (and therefore persuasive) argument. My answer came out as a word salad, despite my best intentions.

This is my "do over."

"These are tough times in construction. Can we really afford to do more than is minimally required?"

Tough times are among the best times to take to the high road.

Ethical leadership is not about altruism. The student's question underscores precisely why this is so: because altruism is fragile and times can be tough. An enlightened perspective on self-interest, by contrast, is both durable and timeless. Such a perspective leads us to invest in strong, strategic commercial relationships. Those relationships are at the heart of any meaningful conception of social responsibility or ethical leadership.

When we think about social responsibility, we think about relationships with stakeholders – the people who touch a business and without whom that business cannot prosper. Stakeholders include shareholders and employees, customers, vendors, partners, and the broader community. The socially responsible business leader is committed to ethical conduct with respect to these stakeholders. The smart leader is also committed to investing in stakeholder relationships in ways that pay off for everyone involved. This isn't altruism, it is good business.

In tough times, strong stakeholder relationships become more important, not less. It is more important to develop strategic vendor relationships when some businesses are failing and others are straining to honor their commitments. In an environment of layoffs, employees are often asked to do more with less. It becomes more important, therefore, to retain the right people and to sustain their motivation and commitment. The value of customer relationships is obvious, at any time, but especially when they are fewer and purchases smaller. In all of these cases, the biggest single factor is trust. Trust increases the speed and reduces the cost of commerce.

We build trust by choosing partners who are trustworthy and by being trustworthy ourselves. Communicate early and often, honestly and clearly. Listen carefully to what people need and seek ways to meet those needs. Be willing to make commitments and be dogged in honoring them. When circumstances intervene, communicate some more. Make sure that employees share in the vision of the organization

– both embracing it and participating in shaping it. The same could be said, in different ways, with respect to vendors and customers. If we are honest about "all being in this thing together," and genuinely act in ways that promote trust and build relationships, we will all be stronger for it.

There may be another silver lining, as well. Building trust need not be costly, at least in terms of cash outlay. In fact, expectations for cash outlays might actually be lower when everyone feels the pressure. So, non-cash measures take on new meaning. Think about creative ways to exceed customer expectations and reward employees. Reinforce that your organization remains committed to excellence. When business is slow, it may be an excellent time to invest in longer-term partnership initiatives and build internal capabilities that will accelerate growth as circumstances change.

Yes, smart businesses absolutely do the right thing, even in a recession. They leverage the power of trust, and build relationships to help them weather the current storm and build toward a brighter future.

—⟋⟍—

Conversation Starters:

Social responsibility and ethical conduct have the potential to drive business performance through improved trust and stronger relationships. This strategy is viable in any business climate.

- Do you do business informed by a clear set of values and principles?
- Is it harder to uphold your values and principles when times are tough? How do you face those challenges?
- If you work in the public sector, what specific ethical challenges do you face "in tough times?" How do you address them?

Lessons Learned

"For God's sake, let us sit upon the ground
And tell sad stories of the death of kings. "
- William Shakespeare, *The Life and Death of Richard the Second,* Act 3,
Scene 2.

April 2011

This past week, I learned that a friend and mentor, Christian Bredo Berghoff, passed away some months ago. Our world is a slightly darker place without Chris, and I wish to share a bit of what I learned from his words and his work.

Chris Berghoff liked to describe himself as a peddler. He was also an entrepreneur, executive, and educator. In 1985 he founded Control Products, Inc., and led it to international prominence as a designer and manufacturer of electronic components for industrial equipment in multiple industries. (The firm is now a part of Emerson Climate Technologies.) Control Products' sustained success was driven in large part by its founder's commitment and strategy: he built trust-based relationships on the basis of honorable conduct and faithful performance. He was also a pretty good salesperson.

As much as any business leader I have known, Berghoff exhibited Ethical Leaders in Action's Virtues of Ethical Leadership: *Service,*

Competence, Creativity, Clarity, and Courage. He practiced each of these, with great success.

Control Products succeeded by turning arms-length customers into shared-destiny, strategic allies. It did so by being uncommonly open and honest, by establishing clear, mutual expectations, and by demonstrating the capacity to innovate and execute. With its allies, the firm created, captured and shared real commercial value based on trust. Chris extended that same commitment to openness and shared success with his employees, hiring with great care, investing in his people's ongoing development and ensuring that the workplace was often a place for fun, as well. He was always "cultivating his farm team," building relationships with professionals he would hire when the time was right. He was almost as proud of Control Products' one-hole "golf course" and employee fitness facilities as he was of its customer list or lab facilities.

Doing business as Chris did – working with clients to create value through innovation – required courage and creativity. It also required clarity and competence to identify opportunities, avoid pitfalls, and solve the problems that inevitably arose for a technology-oriented global enterprise. Chris's commitment to do business that way, and to engage and reward employees in so doing, also reflected his deep sense of service to others. He was a cheerful capitalist who sought to share benefit with the stakeholders of his enterprise.

Chris was also a gifted and enthusiastic educator, teaching for many years at the University of Saint Thomas's Opus College of Business. He presented to varied audiences, including a couple of events for the Hill Center for Ethical Business Leadership, the organization I was leading when I met Chris. While he regarded his ethical practices as a competitive advantage, Chris was nonetheless eager to share them with others – advancing the practices of ethical business leadership one class, one audience, one leader at a time. The Minneapolis *Star Tribune* obituary stated simply, "He was a valued business mentor to hundreds of students and colleagues." I am proud to count myself among them.

I am less proud of a final lesson that Chris taught me, however indirectly. Over the past year, I tried to reach Chris to tell him about my current firm, Ethical Leaders in Action. When he didn't respond, I found myself making any number of assumptions. Most were more about me than about him. I now realize that he was quite busy: fighting cancer, caring for his family, participating in his community, and securing the future of his business. Lesson learned, again. I miss him.

—∿—

Conversation Starters:
Mentors can teach us by example and by helping us to learn from their experiences as well as our own. Mentorship is a remarkable gift.

- Who are your mentors?
- What do you learn from them, and how do you apply it in your work?
- How do you stay connected with them, and why?
- Have you ever thanked your mentors and teachers for their contributions to your life?

Nice Guys: Time to Finish First!

May 2012

The headline from a recent *Harvard Business Review* <u>HBR Daily Stat</u> offered a grim assessment: "*Male Professionals with Higher Ethical Standards Earn Less.*" According to research by Andrew Hussey of the University of Memphis, "Male business professionals who self-report high ethical character earn, on average, **3.4 percent less** than their peers who don't report having such standards." Women suffer no such penalty. Furthermore, men who report that their MBA education raised their ethical standards earn **6.5 percent lower** wages than men who do not. By contrast, women who report that their MBA program raised their ethical standards earned an average of **5.5 percent *more*** than those who did not.

What to make of this?

I'm not going to make the broad case for moral motivation. If you care only about commercial outcomes, I am not going to convince you to change your values and priorities. If you do chose to lead a work life that is both successful and honorable, however, then we have much to discuss and this research should be of interest to you, as it is to me.

We might be tempted to see this finding as just another example of "nice guys finishing last." That would be a mistake. If we take the research at face value, then men who see themselves as having high ethical standards, and especially those who feel that their business education bolstered those standards, are earning somewhat less than those who don't feel that way. This doesn't mean that moral apathy pays. It means that those who are morally motivated ought to develop the capabilities to monetize that motivation. Being a "nice guy" – or, to be more precise, an intentionally good person – represents an investment, and recognizing its return requires both will and skills.

Understood in this way, the research reveals a tremendous opportunity: many morally motivated leaders can learn to turn those good intentions into better business performance. Moral motivation can be monetized primarily by building trust-based relationships, and by igniting engagement in employees and other stakeholders. Trust creates efficiencies, starting with reduced contracting and compliance costs. It also creates an environment for innovation and creativity, supported by sensible, shared risk-taking and open discussion of mutual opportunities and needs. When we trust one another, we seek to do better, together. Engagement, likewise, represents the difference between employees who merely comply with orders and those who cooperate in pursuit of shared goals. The difference, like its payoff, should be obvious.

Consider the following as starting points:

- **Invest in trust-based relationships with customers and vendors.** Establish clear, reasonable ground rules for all. Then seek specific opportunities to turn arms-length, transactional relationships into shared-destiny, strategic partnerships. Understand the needs of your trading partners, and look for the synergies, along with innovation opportunities.

- **Pay particular attention to employees, creating environments that promote cooperation rather than mere compliance.** Driving engagement isn't magic, but with the right efforts, it can work like magic – especially where customer service, productivity, and innovation are concerned. Supervisors can start to reap these benefits by establishing clear performance expectations and by showing that they genuinely care for all team members.

- **Don't forget the "blocking and tackling" of leadership:** sound communication techniques such as active listening, giving direction that focuses on intent and outcomes rather than tasks, and constructive feedback that demonstrates concern.

In this light, the gender difference revealed by the research is especially interesting. Perhaps, on average, women who believe that their ethical sensibilities are honed through education are better than others – and better than men – at building trust-based relationships. Maybe they are more adept at stimulating and engaging teammates.

—ᴍ—

Conversation Starters:

Rather than debate about whether ethical commitments pay off in general, make your own commitments pay off by building trust-based relationships with the key people who can affect your business.

- Whom do you know who has prospered, personally or economically, from their ethical commitments?
- Can you think of both male and female role models in this regard? What differences have you observed in their leadership styles or strategies?
- In your opinion, does benefitting economically tarnish the moral dimension of acting in a principled manner? Why?

I Said it Once, and I'll Say it Again...

February 2009

Last week I had the pleasure of presenting to the City of Lakes Rotary Club. As business and community leaders, Rotarians don't need much convincing to believe that doing the right thing pays off, and so we can quickly get down to the "hows" and "whens." They are a highly receptive audience when it comes to the core concepts of ethical leadership.

So I did my spiel, got laughs in the right places, and was delighted when hands shot up to ask questions. A theme emerged, which is fast becoming *the* question of 2009: "Are people actually doing this stuff when times are so tough?"

I was beset by an out-of-body experience. I started shouting. I was pounding on a table. I didn't speak in tongues, but I might have come close. Clearly, I feel strongly about this: acting in ways that build trust and ignite engagement pay off, even in tough times. Maybe especially in tough times.

I'm not advocating charity here, and I'm not promoting fluff. I am arguing for doing the right thing, in ways that make businesses stronger. Now is an outstanding time to strengthen relationships with customers, vendors, employees, and with all the other people who touch your business. In tough times, great leaders get creative. Now is the time to meet with customers to really understand how you can serve them better, and how you can create more value and capture it

Charles A. Weinstein Ph.D.

for your mutual benefit. If your vendors, in turn, want to serve you better, help them to do so. If they don't seem to care, perhaps there are others who would. Now is the time for all of us to sharpen our games, and work together to achieve what we cannot achieve on our own.

I know I've said this kind of thing before, even in these pages. During this talk, though, people got it. Their attention was palpable. (I am not certain whether it was the substance of my oration or a growing concern that I was having a stroke, but in any case, I had them). I've already had several subsequent conversations, and it is fun to learn how these ideas are actually working:

- A lawyer told of his firm's commitment to using available hours for *pro bono* work now, to maintain staffing levels for when business improves.
- An electronics firm has used its available engineering resources, partnering with a vendor to revamp its environmental practices. The company covered the costs by obtaining concessions from its current vendors in exchange for longer-term contracts. They'll share the ongoing savings with those vendors, as well.
- A component manufacturer faced shutdown when its key customer, a heavy equipment manufacturer, idled plants. Recognizing that end users were keeping their old equipment rather than buying new, they partnered with a distributor to market a new line of spare parts to keep the old machines running.

—\~—

Conversation Starters:
There are many examples of business decisions that are both excellent ethically and excellent commercially.

- Do you have a story to share about doing the right things and making your business stronger?
- Do you think people became more convinced about the effectiveness of this approach during the long U.S. recession?
- What else have we learned during this latest stretch of challenging economic times?

Learning over Corned Beef: My
Great-Uncle's Professional Wisdom

March 2008

Sheldon Weinstein, my great-uncle and an important influence in my adult life, recently passed away at age 84. He was a chartered life underwriter (CLU), in addition to being a husband, father, grandfather, and an intensely interested – if understated – family patriarch. Sheldon was also a great supporter of my work. Beginning shortly after my own father passed away, Sheldon and I began having long lunches on a regular basis, frequently at delicatessens. As I reflect upon these many conversations with him, some interesting and relevant themes emerge.

As a life insurance underwriter, Sheldon took tremendously seriously his obligation to act in his clients' best interest. Sheldon regarded himself as a professional, an underwriter obliged to act in his clients' interest first and foremost. He discharged his professional obligation through extensive, ongoing product research and with great attention to each client's situation. He sold only products, in which he strongly believed, to clients who he believed would benefit from them. He was slow to reach that conclusion and quick to recuse himself when he did not believe his products or expertise were optimally suited to a prospective client. Commercially, Sheldon was not a ball of fire. That wasn't important to him. He was, without fail, a deeply honorable businessman, and this was intensely important to him.

At Sheldon's suggestion, I included in my doctoral research the Code of Ethics of The American Society of Chartered Life Underwriters.[7] My writing led us to some very interesting discussions about what constitutes a profession, and what that designation means in terms of responsibilities. I shall spare you a potentially agonizing summary; suffice it to say that my work benefited greatly from Sheldon's insights.

While he was entirely supportive, Sheldon did not approve of all aspects of my work. Most notably, he was highly critical of my decision to focus not on ethical compliance but on performance-oriented aspects of social responsibility. His oft-repeated criticism took two forms. First, he felt that where corporate malfeasance is concerned, there can never be too many watchdogs. Beyond violating the law, greed and bad faith enraged him, and he thought that there could be no higher calling than to try to curb the worst instincts of fellow businesspeople. I agree with him that compliance is critically important, but I did not see a unique contribution to be made in that arena. Excellent resources exist for businesses interested in creating codes, processes, practices, and cultures that promote ethical conduct.

Second, Sheldon argued that I was misguided in my desire to celebrate and promote excellent business conduct. He was not a fan, for instance, of the stories I tell highlighting businesses that have achieved business gains by investing in stakeholder relationships. When I discussed some of these stories with him, he responded with a question: "Why give people a parade for doing what should simply be expected of them?" That summed up his view.

Reasonable people may disagree (especially when they are both named Weinstein). It isn't merely a matter of catching more flies with honey than with vinegar. (Besides, we all know you can catch the most flies with horse manure.) Developing and implementing strategies that are both commercially successful and socially responsible is a rewarding, if challenging, undertaking. Sharing real-world stories of

---

[7] Now known as the Society of Financial Services Professionals. www.financialpro.org

business successes has become a regular feature of my keynote and workshop presentations.

At bottom, we agreed that good conduct does pay off, financially as well as personally. Sheldon's clients trusted him absolutely because he earned that trust throughout his career. Trust promotes loyalty and referrals. Trust-based relationships form the basis for addressing problems that arise in ways that minimize damage, and for capitalizing on positive opportunities in ways that maximize shared benefits. He may have dismissed this as common sense, but few things are less common or more valuable than an unerring commitment to act in a trustworthy manner.

I miss Uncle Sheldon and I am grateful for all that I learned from his advice, as well as from his example. I expect that I will never eat another corned beef sandwich without thinking of him.

—⁂—

Conversation Starters:

Business and professional ethics encompass both rejecting wrongdoing and embracing a more positive commitment to serve others.

- How much do you care about stopping bad behavior, and why?
- To what extent do you think that free markets reward conduct that exceeds minimum expectations?
- How can leaders in public-sector agencies motivate their teams to exceed stakeholders' expectations?

The Paradox of Shareholder Value

June 2008

In the preceding essays I have argued that a commitment to social responsibility can pay off commercially. Shareholders may be best served when managers make strategic investments in relationships with other stakeholders. Now I intend to go farther: sometimes too much focus on shareholder value creation actually leads to less shareholder value in the long run.

Of course, many business people focus single-mindedly on shareholder value. I have heard some executives describe, with some pride, their "laser-like focus" on intermediate measures such as profits, revenue growth, or both. As business leaders, these folks are too often unsuccessful at driving the very measures they revere. I've worked in various capacities with several firms that were "laser-focused" on generating shareholder value. Some of them were privately held, pursuing the killer initial public offering (IPO). Others were publicly held, trying to boost share price by any means necessary. In nearly every instance, the management teams that single-mindedly focused on shareholder value failed to increase that value. In a couple of instances, shareholder value plummeted – it was like watching a slow-motion train wreck. What was going on there?

Of course, the actual causal factors for business performance are complex, often profoundly so. As managers, we rely on business measures to indicate what's happening in the business. We need data to manage the business, both to predict and to influence outcomes. One problem is, when we start managing the business exclusively by the data points, we lose sight of the complex – and critical – factors that drive real business outcomes.

Metaphors are roaring in my ears right now: a pilot who stares intently at the altimeter, the compass, and the artificial horizon, while she flies her plane into a mountain. Stephen Covey's famous story about the lumberjacks who worry about how quickly they can fell trees until one of them climbs a tree and shouts out, "We're in the wrong forest!" The Three Mile Island nuclear power plant engineers focusing on one set of gauges, worrying about pressure or something, while a stuck valve and dropping water levels almost melt down the reactor. All of these are interesting and instructive analogies, but there is something deeper and more interesting going on here, as well.

To illustrate my point, please bear with me through some old-fashioned philosophy. I promise to make it worthwhile. You may recall that hedonism is the view that pleasure is good. Ethical hedonism (the classic author here is Jeremy Bentham, 1748-1832) is the view that an action is morally right to the extent that it generates the most possible pleasure overall. The particulars vary – distribution of pleasure, what kinds of pleasure, etc. – but a hedonist is someone who acts to maximize pleasure. The egoistic (let's just say selfish) hedonist is someone who seeks to maximize his own pleasure.

Here's an interesting dilemma: *If you focus single-mindedly on maximizing your own pleasure, you are unlikely to achieve that goal over time.* For one thing, if you think about your actions only in terms of how much pleasure they will generate, you will forego the pleasures of spontaneity, of being delighted without seeking it. You may also waste a lot of time simply deciding what to do. More important, great pleasures such as relationships just don't work that way. If you are entirely focused on your own pleasure, you will likely have trouble being an excellent friend, partner, spouse, or parent. These relationships inherently require that we suspend our own pleasure-seeking and make commitments to others. They also deliver unique and remarkable pleasures not otherwise obtainable. And, making your critical commitments contingent upon their pleasure-delivery potential doesn't work. Finally, it is hard to know, in advance, how pleasurable an activity or experience will be. Nothing is more pleasant than a pleasant surprise. As a practical matter, it is difficult or impossible to predict the degree to which our actions will result in pleasure, and our very attempts to do so often diminish the very pleasure we seek to maximize.

Contemporary philosophers, including Peter Railton and others, have called this *"the paradox of hedonism."* I believe a closer look at this paradox can be instructive for business leaders.

Think about the course of our lives. It is easy to imagine that the most pleasurable life is one that includes a host of commitments that are not driven directly by their potential to deliver pleasure. These certainly include the kinds of significant relationships I noted above. Likewise, our spiritual lives, our work lives, and our other passions and commitments can be deeply meaningful and afford us enormous pleasure. We can experience those kinds of pleasures only by thinking about other things first.

So it is in business, as well. By single-mindedly pursuing shareholder value, we put that very outcome in jeopardy. The reasons for this are not surprising. Businesses succeed by delivering value to customers, consistently and efficiently. A business leader who focuses on strengthening the organization's ability to do so, paying appropriate attention to a well-designed set of metrics, will do far better than a leader who focuses only on a narrow set of metrics or outcomes such as stock price.

Moreover, because it is often especially difficult to predict how specific actions will affect shareholder value, undue focus on that end point can lead us to make short-sighted decisions that will not make our organizations better at generating real value. We succumb to the temptation to invest in promotion or hype aimed at attracting or stimulating shareholder interest. In the worst cases, we organize our businesses specifically to be attractive to shareholders, rather than to customers. We think about revenue multiples and scalability before thinking about value propositions and core-business effectiveness and efficiencies. We are better off building our businesses to serve customers by whatever means we have chosen as our strategic direction. Very often, we can generate real shareholder value most effectively by thinking about other things first.

—⚬⚬—

Conversation Starters:

The most pleasurable life is one that involves commitments which are not based on personal pleasure-seeking. The best way to generate shareholder value is to focus in part on other factors, such as customer value.

- Have you fallen victim to the paradox of hedonism, wondering about enjoying your life so much that you forget to enjoy it?
- Can you think of organizational examples that illustrate this paradox?
- Can you think of other instances where the best way to achieve one goal is to focus on another?

The Socially Responsible Barber

December 2007

I am basically a bald guy. This is a revelation only to me – the expansion of my forehead has been steady and entirely visible to all. Still, the power of denial is strong. It is undeniably chilly up there these days.

The darkest irony: less hair necessitates more haircuts. If I don't keep it neatly trimmed, I end up looking like Dilbert's pointy-haired boss.[8] It is fortunate, then, that I am very fond of my barber, Greg. His technical skills are excellent, but more importantly, he's a pleasure to see every few weeks, and a source of informed opinion on a wide range of topics.

Enough about me

This is not a shameless plug for Greg (and I'd rather not think about plugs in my sensitive state).[9] Rather, Greg and I have been discussing – you guessed it – ethical leadership during our increasingly-frequent meetings. Last time, Greg raised some interesting questions. Essentially, he wanted to know whether all this social responsibility stuff might be of any value to him, a self-employed barber. How could his extremely small business profitably apply the principles we are developing and espousing?

[8] Enjoy Scott Adams's Dilbert comic strips at www.dilbert.com. Live them in almost any workplace where humans gather.

[9] I don't mind giving credit where credit is due. Greg's Website is gregzrust.com. In 2014 as this book goes to press, Greg is still my barber, a job which is even less demanding than it was when this was when this essay first appeared online in 2007.

As we have noted, I tend to think of social responsibility in terms of stakeholder relationships. Specifically, the key questions concern how well sound ethical principles are embedded in the organization and the degree to which those principles guide an organization's actions with respect to its stakeholders (those whom the organization touches). Stakeholders include owners and shareholders, as well as employees, customers, vendors, partners, and the communities in which a company does business, including the natural environment. The acme of social responsibility involves creative business strategies that improve relationships with those entities in ways which measurably benefit the business. Can we sensibly apply this approach to a self-employed barber? The suspense is killing you, isn't it?

Of course we can! Stakeholder relationships and social responsibility become especially relevant as we look for ways to sustain and grow those very small businesses. So as not to embarrass Greg, let's consider how a hypothetical colleague, Sandy the Stylist, might grow her business.

The stylist and stakeholder relationships

Sandy is self-employed, renting space from a salon. She shares walk-in business and does her turn at the chores, but otherwise is on her own. As we shall see, Sandy has some opportunities to invest in social responsibility in ways that pay off. We shall begin with the obvious stakeholder, the customer. There are many opportunities to explore:

- **The experience of a haircut goes well beyond the haircut itself.** Are Sandy's salon surroundings appealing to her target customer? To her actual customers? How well does Sandy know what her customers want, and what they merely tolerate? Does she try to enhance their experiences?
- **Lots of people have very personal relationships with barbers.** Are they handled with mutual trust? Appropriate discretion? Genuine concern?
- **Conflicts and problems are sure to arise.** Does Sandy have clear, fair policies for situations like no-shows, or work that is not satisfactory? If handled properly, an error can be an occasion for building, rather than damaging, a customer relationship.

More generally, Sandy can capture the business value of her efforts through improved customer satisfaction, retention and referrals. These are easily measured, and they are the keys to her business. In fact, as Sandy builds stronger relationships with customers, she should call on them to give her candid feedback to help her continue to improve her business.

While Sandy doesn't have employees, she does have vendors, including product suppliers and the salon owner from whom she rents space. She both cooperates and competes with that owner and with her other salon-mates. Basic rules of fairness should govern these relationships, but there might also be some written terms to assure clarity and mutual understanding. When problems or tensions arise, there should be candid, constructive conversations to address and resolve them. Does Sandy take the lead in resolving conflicts and finding win-win solutions to problems? Do Sandy and her salon owner have a clear understanding – in writing – about how revenues and costs are divided?

Environmental responsibility

The environment as a stakeholder is a hot topic, for good reasons. Sandy may have considerable opportunities to green up her practice:

- Selecting and using environmentally friendly products – not necessarily the highly-hyped ones. There are many green options in health and beauty products.
- Reducing waste, perhaps by sharing perishable products with salon-mates or simply by minding consumption.
- Using bulk products or those that feature environmentally friendly packaging.
- Advising customers of ways to "go green" in their health and beauty regimens.

Sandy can probably recoup the cost of her efforts simply by reducing waste. She can also market her services to customers who truly care about the environment.

We can all take time to support the community, but for someone in Sandy's position, time is truly money. Getting involved in community activities that are of interest to her will yield networking opportunities to grow her business. She can make charitable contributions that result in marketing exposure (such as sponsoring a blog on commercially-savvy social responsibility). She can spend some of that chair time sharing worthy events of interest to her customers. She might even use her Website to highlight worthy social causes or upcoming events of interest to her customers. Low cost stuff, with the potential for reasonably high impact.

My point should be obvious by now: almost anyone in business can find ways to integrate socially responsible practices into their business, in ways that will pay off commercially while they benefit society. It isn't about becoming a paragon of virtue. It is about creativity and commitment to ongoing improvement.

—m—

Conversation Starters:
Even the smallest businesses can benefit from a thoughtful commitment to social responsibility.

- Do you think it's more difficult for a self-employed stylist (or other small business) or a large company to operate in a socially responsible manner?
- Who are the stakeholders in your business or organization and how do you invest in them? Does it pay off?
- Can you think of new ideas for you or your company to do more in the realm of social responsibility that also serves the bottom line?

Airborne!

August 2012

I will conclude the "Emerging Perspective" section as I conclude many of my speeches, with the following story.

Recently, a good friend took me flying in a single-engine Piper. It was great fun, and, in a very distinctive way, quite thought-provoking.

I am not a pilot. Understandably then, I considered myself a passenger, useful only as ballast. The pilot corrected me: I was crew. I needed to understand what was going on in the cockpit, and how the critical systems worked. I needed to be able to assist. We began by completing a very thorough pre-flight checklist, examining the aircraft and testing systems inside and out. We discussed basic emergency procedures.

We launched into a bright, still morning sky, climbing to around 3,000 feet. Flying at that altitude retains an intimacy with the landscape not found on commercial flights. While I was enjoying the view, the pilot was scouting locations for emergency landings, teaching me what to look for and explaining what must happen in the unlikely event of a power failure. We turned toward our first destination, the airport in St. Cloud, Minnesota.

As we made our way northwest, the pilot turned the controls over to me. I have flown a few times under similar circumstances with other pilot friends, and was thrilled to have the opportunity. I am not ashamed to admit that my exuberance far exceeded my competence. The plane flew in what the pilot politely called "S-turns," unintentional squiggles across the sky. It was surprisingly difficult to keep the aircraft flying in the desired direction at the desired altitude.

Then the pilot delivered the critical correction: "Loosen your grip on the yoke. Fly with your fingertips." It made all the difference. With a little intentional subtlety, I was able to fly straight and level. With occasional course corrections for wind, we flew smoothly toward our destination. Ultimately, it felt like sailing a small boat, but in three dimensions.

I flew again on the return leg. On the way out, I relied primarily on the instruments. This time, I tried to actually use the windshield. What I found was quite surprising: I couldn't reliably sense our altitude and direction changes without the instruments. My body and senses deceived me. I have read about this phenomenon, which is a cause of many small plane crashes, but to actually feel it was pretty jarring. At one point, as I looked out the window at the St. Croix River for just a few moments, the aircraft almost completely got away from me, climbing and turning rather sharply, despite my intention to maintain a steady course. Lesson learned: flying requires constant attention.

What other lessons can we learn?

First, in any line of work it is worth asking whether we regard ourselves—or treat our teammates – as passengers or as crew. Being crew definitely kept my head in the game. I was fully engaged, and even though I was not in charge, I felt jointly responsible for our shared endeavor.

The experience also brought to mind my favorite sailing metaphor: it requires a strong, steady hand to make the ongoing small adjustments necessary to steer a straight course. It is often tempting to over-control, and easy to over-correct. The results are rarely consistent with our intentions.

Further, course adjustments are never-ending. Leadership, like piloting, requires sustained attention. People, teams, and organizations stray while leaders are looking elsewhere, confident that they have communicated their intent to others who are executing. There is no substitute for ongoing attention and communication.

By the same token, we need outside input to make sound decisions. Our perceptions, like our senses, can deceive us. We are inherently limited by our own perspective, and can only overcome that limitation by engaging others, and by establishing measures – our instruments – that provide critical, objective input to our decision-making.

Finally, our safety was protected not just by our pilot's competence, but also by his sustained vigilance and reliance on sound processes. We are all human. Consistent practices, sound processes, and tools such as checklists prevent lapses in an environment that is ultimately unforgiving. Like business, for example.

A recreational airplane ride turned out to be a fairly intense experience. It was also immensely enjoyable. That's no surprise: we all know that meaningful challenges can be great fun.

—m—

Conversation Starters:
Being a crew member is nearly always more rewarding than just going along for the ride.
- On the teams with which you work, do you consider yourself a passenger, or a crew member?
- When you are in charge, do you engage team members as crew, or just bring them along for the ride?
- Can you think of ways to cultivate the strong, steady hand required to make the continual small adjustments that your organization's success requires?

Part II

On Living Like a Grown-Up

I am in my mid-40s. When I look in the mirror, I no longer feel like I am pretending to be a grown-up, like I'm wearing my father's suit. In fact, I have shoes that are older than I was when I last felt that way.

I am already far more like my father than I ever intended to be. It isn't that I didn't admire my dad – quite the contrary. (The first essay in this section is about him.) It is just that adulthood seemed to come on when I wasn't looking. Fifteen minutes ago I was in my early 20s, feeling fairly certain that I already knew everything I needed to know. Now I am at times nearly overwhelmed by all that I have yet to learn. Nevertheless, people seem to treat me like I am an adult. At this, I continue to marvel.

That is not to say that I don't, at times, act in a less than adult manner. In this, I know that I am not alone. We are all human beings, and we are all capable of acting selfishly, impulsively, or otherwise immaturely. Two questions to ponder are what constitutes maturity, and how does it relate to traditional moral concepts like virtue and integrity. A therapist friend once proposed that one way to explain much of organizational dynamics is to expect individuals to think and act like adolescents much of the time. I find that analysis troubling, but I must admit that it explains many of the problems that arise when people try to work together. Perhaps a more fundamental question is, how can we spend more of our lives doing far better than that? How can we better strive to act responsibly, or even honorably?

These essays address questions of how we can live our lives as responsible adults. I also wonder (and write about) how we can remain childlike in important ways: how we can continue to wonder, to question, and to play with all of our hearts.

Father's Day

June 2012

My father, Maher J. Weinstein, died of cancer nearly two decades ago. I think of him every day. Maher was a lawyer by profession, but a teacher by disposition. He was also a remarkable human being who enjoyed the hell out of his own life, while enriching the lives of many who knew him.

I was 25 years old when my dad died. At times I feel fortunate to have had an adult relationship with him, however brief, and to have learned from him throughout my early life. Other times I feel utterly robbed. This afternoon, my wife Cathy and I took the kids pan fishing. It was a perfect moment for my own parents to have enjoyed, but for their untimely deaths.

In my situation, I feel certain that Maher would have dismissed the matter of fairness, and focused on the positive. He didn't expect life to be fair. In fact, he was fond of declaring that "The Fair is on Como Avenue once a year." He knew how to live in the moment, and especially how to find humor, comfort, and pleasure in the things he could control. He laughed early and often, and told even the moldiest jokes with infectious enthusiasm. Thick steaks and excellent Scotch – or sausages and cold beer, in accordance with his circumstances – were also among his go-to pleasures. In his honor I have cultivated an excellent relationship with a local butcher shop, and I respect their skill and commitment as much as he would have.

Maher respected and enjoyed people, not merely for their skills. He embraced respect as an ethic: Everyone is entitled to respect, he argued, and respect is not to be confused with affection. He looked down on the cruel, the scuzzy, and the crooked – but just about nobody else. As a lawyer he tended to help people solve problems and, when possible, to resolve conflicts and rebuild relationships. He cared more about helping people than he did about getting paid. While there was certainly some financial cost to some of his professional choices, there was also a much deeper payoff: I am certain that he enjoyed serving clients by applying artfulness, intellect, or insight much more than he enjoyed any corresponding fees.

Finally, from my father I learned that nearly everyone has something to teach us. He listened, he asked questions, and he collected and shared stories. By the same token, one of the greatest pleasures of my work is the opportunity to learn from others. Sometimes this comes directly through active listening. Often, we learn together through collaboration over time. People, in turn, tend to take pleasure in being listened to, and in learning together. Many, perhaps all of us, hunger to be respected and appreciated. Learning is arguably the ultimate win-win interaction. On my best days, I take great pleasure in learning from others specifically because of all that I learned from my dad.

—⁊⁊⁊—

Conversation Starters:
Some of us are fortunate to have parents who are also teachers and role models. We may not want to be them, but we certainly want to cultivate their best aspects in ourselves.
- What did your parents teach you about how to live?
- We can learn from positive and negative examples. How have you adapted these lessons to make them your own?
- What lessons do we seek to teach those around us?

Let's Hear it for the Amateurs

May 2012

I have spent much of the past few weeks delivering half-day train-ing programs to groups of fire service leaders brought together from multiple departments.[10] The concentrated repetition of topics, together with the diverse audiences (many departments, all levels of experience) have stimulated some new ideas, and challenged me to hone some of my established content.

One new insight arose from an extended discussion of the different skills and passions required to do great work in the fire service: fire chiefs and trainers across the country are rightly focused on professionalism. However, there is a great deal to be said for the spirit of amateurism, as well. Understood correctly, amateurism is as important to the fire service as professionalism. The fire service is not unique in this regard.

Professionalism entails cultivating key skills, sound judgment, and a level-headed commitment to duty. These are indeed necessary quali-ties in our first responders and those who lead them. The same holds

---

[10] Some of this work was under the auspices of the Gasaway Consulting Group. I'm grateful to Rich Gasaway for his friendship and collaboration on a number of profes-sional engagements. www.richgasaway.com

true for many other worthy endeavors. Fire service leaders rightly seek to be recognized and respected as professionals.

When we use the term, "amateur," by contrast, it often carries only negative connotations: a lack of skill, or a less-than-full-time level of commitment. That is a mistake. The great strength of amateurism is revealed by its linguistic roots; the word originates from the Latin for to love, *amare*. An amateur is one who is driven by a love for the work. Indeed, it takes great passion and a desire for community service to do the work of the fire service really well, from answering midnight pages to treating even difficult customers with respect and compassion. To love the job means working with passion and intrinsic motivation. To be an amateur, in the purest sense, takes nothing away from professionalism.

Wise folks do not take love for granted. This should also apply to the spirit of amateurism. Thus, we need to foster organizations, teams, and working conditions that promote love of the job. If we make it onerous to answer the call to duty, fewer will do so. If our teams marginalize or isolate individuals, they squander the passions of those individuals, at everyone's expense. Too often, I have seen firefighters or officers turn away from their teams when a misunderstanding goes unaddressed, or when an isolated mistake becomes a topic of ridicule. The team members involved may not say anything; they might just show up less often, and respond less passionately. It is worth asking what might be inhibiting our teammates' passion for the job, and worth looking into our own hearts for evidence of the same inhibitions. A little attention to these matters can go a long way toward returning people to doing and feeling their best.

Unfortunately, we tend to link the perception of professionalism with compensation. In the fire service, there is an enduring tension between part-time (sometimes volunteer, often paid-on-call) and career firefighters. Misperceptions abound. Some hold that volunteer personnel are less skilled, while others hold that career personnel see their service as nothing more than a job. As measures of reality, these generalizations don't hold up: plenty of part-time responders are exceedingly capable, and plenty of career responders are as passionate as anyone donning turnout gear (or a Sparky the Dog suit at an education event, for that matter).

For our purposes, those stereotypes are accidentally instructive. They remind us that ethical leaders must display the talent, sound judgment, and sense of duty that we associate with professionals and the passion and sense of community that animate the best amateurs. *We should cultivate and celebrate both professionalism and passion, and take care that our pursuit of one does not inhibit the other.*

By recognizing the compelling power of love for the job, we can be more conscious about cultivating it. We can also address those practices, behaviors, or habits that make it harder for people to love their jobs or to feel connected with their teams and communities. We can see that these are costly mistakes, and we can take decisive action to correct them.

Let us all seek to be our best: as passionate professionals, and as skilled, dutiful amateurs. Let us create and maintain environments that promote excellence and love for the job.

—∿—

Conversation Starters:
We need to challenge and integrate our traditional concepts of "amateurism" and "professionalism." The best performers exhibit passion, skill, knowledge, and a commitment to service regardless of compensation.

- What animates you in your work? What tends to squelch your enthusiasm?
- Compare your attitude toward career-related work with your attitude toward a hobby or avocation. What can we learn from that comparison?
- What can you do to stir the passions of those around you (for work!)?

Make Mistakes with Class

September 2013

We human beings are fallible. We make mistakes. Screw up. Goof. Err. Given that errors are inevitable, I'm always surprised by how painful it can be to face that aspect of our humanity.

A healthy respect for our fallibility is a very good thing. It causes us to be careful, and to design processes and objects that respect our human shortcomings. Fail-safe systems exist simply because, well, systems fail. With that in mind, we proceed with caution. We may learn to work together, in ways that shore up our shortcomings. We get better, and we minimize the inevitable errors along the way.

Sometimes that respect turns to fear, and that's not always such a good thing. Fear of making mistakes can paralyze us. It can lead us to avoid acceptable risks, foregoing desirable outcomes. In other words, we don't go for it, so we don't succeed. Even if we are able to muster our courage, the fear can make us tense and less focused – again, less likely to succeed in the long run. Most troubling, perhaps, is the desire to hide or cover up our mistakes. There's almost no mistake that can't be made worse by covering it up afterward. Fear of making mistakes, beyond a healthy respect, can only make us less effective.

So, I propose that we embrace our fallibility, and learn to make mistakes with class. This means:

1. Be accountable for our mistakes. Own our errors, and make a sincere effort to mitigate any harm we've caused.
2. Learn from our mistakes. Don't repeat them.
3. Forgive ourselves and move on with our lives.

Making mistakes with class not only helps us recover from our missteps; it helps us avoid the fear that can actually bring on more errors, or worse ones.

Learning from our mistakes takes place both individually and organizationally. Perhaps I was scared, or overconfident, or lazy. I can address that. Perhaps there was information that I didn't have, which I needed. Health care organizations in particular are getting better at seeing individual mistakes as markers of broader weaknesses, in training, in processes, or even in organizational cultures. Not examining our mistakes to see what we can learn squanders a valuable opportunity to get better.

Here's another benefit of making mistakes with class: It sets a tone that allows others to do so, as well. Too often, our workplaces feature cultures in which people are overcautious, even paralyzed, or where fear of embarrassment increases the temptation to cover up mistakes. Nobody benefits from that. Let us lead by example, showing that even duly cautious people make mistakes, and respond to them like effective adults. By owning our mistakes, learning from them, and then forgiving ourselves and moving on, we can actually reduce errors and increase our ability to respond to the remaining issues at the same time.

—⚍—

Conversation Starters
Making mistakes is inevitable. Make them with class!

- What are some things that you have learned from your mistakes?
- Have you ever had something not work out as planned, but turn out to be excellent in its own way?

- Have you made certain past mistakes a part of your identity? Are you prepared to let them go and forgive yourself?
- Think about an instance when a mistake made an individual, team, or organization stronger. What can we learn from your story?

The Ranting Tree: A Shortage of Wise Adults

July 2010

My youngest child, not yet 2 years old, has discovered Shel Silverstein's *The Giving Tree*. "Tree! "Tree!" He begs, pleads, and ultimately demands. I have read it to him four times today. It was a light day.

I hate *The Giving Tree*. I remember it vaguely from my own childhood, where it was read to me, presumably without incident. More recently, reading it to my own child left me deeply, inconsolably sad. As I thought about it (and given my son's appetite for repetition, I had plenty of time to think about it), sadness turned to anger.

As you may recall, the book is an illustrated poem, telling the story of a relationship between a female tree and "a boy." In the boy's youth, the tree was the center of his abundant free time. The tree was delighted to share her leaves, her apples, and her shade, for the boy's company and the pleasure of his joy. As he grew older, the boy made increasing demands of the tree, who ultimately invited the boy to take everything, leaving the tree with nothing, a stump, utterly alone. The story closes with an elderly "boy" sitting upon the stump, who was again "happy" to be giving to the boy, and to be in the boy's company.

What a terrible story! One character sacrifices herself utterly while the other exploits her. Is Silverstein extolling this relationship as an ideal for love? The debate about this work has gone on since its introduction in 1964. I am cursed to read this story, over and over, to a cheerful toddler...who just takes and takes....

Then I realized that throughout the story, the exploitive character is identified only as "the boy." He is depicted in his youth, in adolescence, through early and late adulthood, and ultimately in very old age. In contrast to the illustration, in the text he remains "the boy." This simple convention reveals the source of my angst.

I am struck by a global shortage of adulthood. Our political debates have devolved to childish oversimplification, name calling, and, all too often, fear mongering. I work with many wonderful (adult) leaders, but I also encounter too many business people – and business students – who try to cover naked selfishness and short-sightedness with a cloak of "market discipline" or "commercial rationality." They seek short-term gains, at all costs. I work with fire and law enforcement officers, some of whom pursue personal agendas or foster petty resentments at the expense of their missions. These individuals don't believe in building trusting relationships, because they are equipped neither to trust nor to earn trust. They are boys and girls, engaged in exploitation.

These traits are acceptable, even unavoidable, in a toddler. Even the tree was equipped to meet the needs of a young child, sustainably. While the "boy's" body and desires grew, he did not mature. He gained neither foresight, nor any concern for the tree's well-being. Adults care for those who love them. Good adults care about the well-being of others, more generally. Wise adults have foresight.

—∿—

Conversation Starters
Young children simply take from others. Good adults care about others, and often care for others.
- What, in your opinion, are the essential features of adulthood?
- Do you see concern for others as a trait that comes with maturity? What promotes or inhibits its expression?
- Why do we seem to have fewer "wise adults" in the world today, and how do you think we can go about changing that?

Of Mountains, Molehills and Change
Management

February 2008

I recently enjoyed a vacation day skiing at a local Minnesota ski area (readers from beyond the Midwest may insert a smug chuckle here). It was my birthday, and in recent years this local ski outing has become something of a habit. It feels good to be outdoors. The business was fine without me.

For whatever reason, I was irrationally nervous as I put on my skis. I took first to the bunny hill, using its scant inertia to propel me to the nearest full-sized chair lift. There was no line on a Monday morning, so I took a moment to ask the lift operator whether "there's an easy way down from this lift."

"Is this your first time on skis?" he asked, clearly surprised by the question.

"No."

"You basically know how to ski?"

"Sure."

He smiled, leaning toward me. "I don't know if you noticed, but we don't actually have a mountain here," he whispered. "You can pretty much ski anywhere you want."

So I did, all day. What was I worried about? I don't really care. I'm just grateful that I was able to relax and enjoy the day.

There's a very personal story here, about my slight inclination toward physical cowardice, and a deep commitment not to let it rule my actions. A more interesting observation, though, concerns the ease with which our fears, both conscious and unconscious, literally create mountains in our imagination. At best, we waste energy preparing to scale mountains that do not exist. At worst, this shadow terrain obscures and prevents us from pursuing our very real objectives.

Is it courageous to realize that our fears are unfounded? Not especially, but it is probably a hallmark of adulthood. It is certainly a leader's task to sort out real and imaginary risks, beginning with our own imaginations.

There are mountains of literature about what is called "change management." That term has always struck me as peculiar, given the more or less constant state of change in most organizations. Isn't "static management" really the exception and "change" the norm? Still, MBA students read Kotter and Schlesinger, Heifetz and Linsky, and a host of other authors, all offering guidance on how to lead others through the process of organizational change. A common theme: overcoming the resistance to change, and addressing the conflicting interests that arise as the players imagine or predict what an upcoming change will mean for them.

Perhaps we can go a long way toward overcoming the overall burden of resistance to change, simply by reminding ourselves and one another – clearly and compassionately – that some mountains are imaginary. We would do well to remember that others may perceive very real challenges that aren't immediately apparent to us. Good conversations can help everyone survey and understand the true landscape of any change. We will be effective in delineating reality, to the extent that we have already earned the trust and respect of our teams. Indeed, the condition of ongoing change offers ample opportunity to build credibility over time.

—w—

<u>Conversation Starters:</u>
Very often, we are held back by barriers that exist largely in our imagination.

- What are the imaginary mountains holding you back?
- What aspects of organizational changes have seemed like mountains? What brought them back to scale?
- What do you think about the opposite problem: minimizing or ignoring an important or urgent issue?

My Ideas

April 2011

I tend to fall in love with my ideas. Let me be clear: I have many ideas, and while some are pretty good, others are frankly unworthy of the affection I might lavish upon them. While ideas are hatching I tend to become attached, cultivating or defending them because I thought of them.

This poses a couple of problems. The first is obvious: wasted time and energy. I fall in love at all stages of an idea's development; a fleeting notion may occupy me as completely as a richly-framed concept. Much time is wasted by my unwillingness to prioritize or – gasp – to edit. It is sometimes very, very noisy in my head.

The second problem is more pernicious: I don't always play well with others. Once I have become attached to an idea, I sometimes have trouble doing what I know is right, i.e., inviting others in to consider, adopt, improve, or implement it. I teach people how to do this for a living. That doesn't mean I find it easy.

There's a fine, sometimes barely visible line between strength and shortcoming. Strong leaders maintain and defend core ideas like vision, objectives and values. Meaningful achievements often require a high degree of resolve (or, less charitably, stubbornness). However, not all achievements are meaningful and sometimes our circumstances demand flexibility, or nimbleness. We learn from experience, and our beliefs should reflect that reality. In almost any situation, our ideas improve through collaboration.

As I work on these traits, I don't think I'm unique, or even unusual. We often see people clinging to ideas, unwilling to adapt or share. In fact, if we never see them, those people are probably us.

The good news: this particular shortcoming generally succumbs to awareness. Once I realize that I'm being intransigent, I can generally relax and open up to others. On a good day, I can laugh at myself. And, I have found no greater tool for awareness than good friends, whom I trust to check my blind spots. In that way, I am fortunate that this trait is often self-correcting, costing little more than wasted time or slight embarrassment. This is yet another benefit of having people who have our backs.

—⁓—

Conversation Starters

It is easy to fall in love with our own ideas, and hard to accept criticism, however constructive and helpful it may be.

- When it comes to your own ideas, do you *fall in love too easily?*[11]
- Can you think of a situation in which falling in love with your own ideas may have been to your detriment?
- In what kinds of situations have you found that resolve/stubbornness were necessary and effective?
- What are some of the ways you have found to make collaboration work?

[11] Apologies to songwriters/lyricists Julie Styne and Sammie Cahn.

King Lear's Lessons for Grown-Ups

June 2009

When our Ethical Leadership Working Group[12] decided to read and watch *King Lear*, my mind went back more than 20 years, to the frustrated words of a particularly memorable English professor: "Mr. Weinstein, I am stunned – not merely disappointed, but stunned – by your prosaic observations and flat-footed arguments. I hope you show more promise as a philosopher than as a literary critic." (I share his hope.) Despite that dark assessment, I now seek to apply *King Lear* to the enterprise of leadership in general, and adulthood in particular. I won't rehash the plot here, when you can find professional summaries all over the Internet. Maybe you remember the story without the crib notes. Suffice it to say that *Lear* is a story of a father with three daughters, and the consequences of two daughters' ill will and his own bad choices. It is a study in human frailty.

Lear's leadership lessons are not as readily accessible as other texts we've tackled in discussion groups. Shakespeare's language is lush and gorgeous, but it can inhibit conceptual understanding among us, the Tweeting Masses. The plot seems a mess, with blinded and semi-naked men stumbling around the countryside, interspersed with

---

[12] This reading and discussion group met monthly for several years, bringing together remarkable people for discussions on a wide range of topics related to ethical leadership. I am so grateful for the input of these thoughtful leaders.

acts of violence and sexual impropriety. Nearly without exception, the characters are distinguished primarily by their weaknesses and flaws. Even the names are confusing.

Not surprisingly, the reader is rewarded for her efforts. I believe that in Lear, we can find lessons in adulthood. Shakespeare presents us with a study in human frailty. We can see our vices, beginning with Lear's own vain and faulty test of his daughters' love for him. That shortcoming is entirely overshadowed by the malicious motives and vile actions of his elder daughters and their respective consorts. It's rough out there, and there are nasty people everywhere. Children require simple, unambiguous, happy endings. Adults can tolerate ambiguity, complexity, and the reality that bad things do happen, and bad people sometimes win.

A starker lesson in adulthood is not about the external world, but about the limits on our ability to change it. Who among us has not, at times, felt put upon by circumstances? We face challenges per-sonal, professional, political and – especially of late – macroeconomic. Adolescents feel bulletproof. When we see that we are mortal, what can we do? Do we fold? Do our very mental faculties desert us? Our character is not defined by what we confront, but by how we confront it and how we respond.

Adults are realistic. A few people hearing my public addresses have accused me of painting too rosy a picture, noting that all of my cited examples of ethical conduct result in organizational success. My firm's underlying message that the good guys can win, they have argued, obscures the reality that sometimes tough decisions need to be made and the results don't always favor the virtuous. I hope I haven't been that lopsided, but I accept the observation and have integrated more cautionary language into my speeches. Virtue doesn't always pay, but through analytical rigor, creativity, and courage, ethical leaders can often win. Often, but not always. It's like the old joke about bear hunting with nothing but a knife: "Sometimes you get the bear, and sometimes the bear gets you." In *King Lear*, the metaphorical bear seems to get everyone.

So, as morally committed adults, we are faced with the challenge of discerning and doing the right things, again and again, without the adolescent belief in our own invincibility or the juvenile certainty that the good guys always win. We can rise to that challenge by taking care of ourselves and one another, acting in ways that reflect a deep concern for the well-being of others. We can support one another in that pursuit, celebrating successes, recovering from failures, and learning from all of it. The world may not be as simple as children imagine, but it is a rich and wonderful place in which we, as adults, can thrive.

—⁓—

Conversation Starters:
Part of being an adult is making hard choices, and living with the consequences.

- When have you had to live with the consequences of a bad choice?
- Do you long for childhood, cherish adulthood, or feel something else altogether? Why?
- What is the most important lesson you have learned that focuses on an aspect of adulthood?

Why? Because...

October2011

"When I give an order, the last thing I want to hear is, `Why?' The *only* thing I want to hear is, `Yes, sir!'" The statement came from a seasoned sheriff, at a gathering of senior law enforcement leaders. His peers rushed to agree. A veteran commander jumped in. "The young ones are the worst. When I was a new cop, I never, ever, ever would have asked why. Ever." Many of the leaders gathered that day shared stories of punishment, sanctioned or unsanctioned, meted out to subordinates of old, who dared to question....

I understand a leader's hesitation when she is asked, "Why?" It is easy to feel like our direction is being questioned, or our leadership doubted. Most often, though, that is not the case. A subordinate may be seeking clarification, trying to understand his leader's thought process in order to faithfully execute her intent. And, whether or not such a question is asked, often the best thing a leader can do is explain her directions as fully as time and circumstances allow.

I direct someone to take action in order to achieve a particular outcome. If circumstances change, or an action doesn't work out as intended, then my subordinate needs to understand my intention in order to bring about the desired outcome. Even better, I can often engage that subordinate as an ally by explaining how the intended actions can bring about something we both value. If, instead, I answer "Why?" with, "Because I said so," I have done nothing to motivate or engage anyone.

"Because I said so" is also disrespectful. That statement simply underscores that the person to whom it is addressed is a subordinate forced to comply, rather than a full person, willing and able to contribute. In which roles are we most likely to see people at their best: as minions, or as contributors? What tone do we wish to set in our organizations?

Finally, by sharing our intent and explaining why our desired ends are worthwhile, we help others to participate in leadership now, and we guide emerging leaders with our thought processes. By being explicit about our intent, we invite others to help improve our thinking, our plans, and our direction. Such explanation also serves as a positive example and instruction for those who are learning to lead and direct others.

There are times and places for terse direction; it is worth noting that this discussion arose among public safety leaders, who function in paramilitary hierarchies designed for emergency response. Even in those contexts, only a very small minority of the work is done under emergent circumstances. Happily, for most of us, these circumstances are even less common. In nearly all cases, when we give direction we ought to share what we intend to bring about, and why it is important. Persuasion and engagement are nearly always more powerful than coercion and compliance.

—ɯ—

Conversation Starters:
Except under rare circumstances, sharing your intent is an important part of giving direction.
- When are you comfortable taking orders? What features distinguish those situations?
- Do you tend to perform better when you are called on to contribute, rather than directed to accomplish a certain task?
- When you are giving direction, do you share your intent? Are you open to questions and discussion?

The Beauty in Potential

March 2012

I t is spring. An enduring international symbol of this season
of rebirth is the cherry blossom, revered in Japan as the *sakura*.
Picnicking under the *sakura* (and before that, the *umi*) tree is an annual celebration that dates back at least 1,500 years. People of all ages
pause to appreciate and to celebrate the blossoms and all that they
represent. Today, let us take a lesson from that practice and the beliefs
that underlie it.

Our best American analog is probably the autumn leaves. As our
newscasters track the locations of "peak fall colors," Japanese newscasters report the advance of the "*sakura* front." Both present beauty that
is spectacular and ephemeral; incandescent leaves fade and fall, and
the softly vibrant blossoms turn to fruit (whether we pause to appreciate them or not). There is an important difference, too: while we treasure autumn woods at their peak of brilliance, the Japanese prize the
sakura blossoms most highly before their peak, when they still have the
inherent potential to become larger or more brilliant. The most beautiful *sakura* blossoms are still becoming even fuller and more striking.

How might we respond to this aesthetic value? Perhaps by celebrating a balance of the realized and the potential in us as individuals,

and especially in teams and organizations. Very often, our efforts to improve are delayed by a belief that we are "already good enough," or thwarted by a deeper fear of criticism. Or, perhaps we are simply too busy to reflect on how we might realize our potential.

In fact, we may choose both to take pride of our achievements, and to dedicate ourselves to improvement. We can celebrate the beauty that we see, while we pursue that which we envision. And we can remember that time is fleeting. If not now, when?

—w—

Conversation Starters
Pause to appreciate both excellence and the potential for improvement.
- When do you find it difficult to acknowledge room for improvement?
- In the workplace, how do we cultivate the skill of recognizing and cultivating potential in colleagues, subordinates…and our leaders?
- Do you have examples of great potential fully realized, or not fully realized? What lessons did you learn from these situations?
- How could we shift our perception of value to be a little more Japanese? Should we?

Bully! Problem and Opportunity

September 2011

During a break in one recent seminar, a group of parents gathered around the refreshments. All had kids in grades 5-8. Many of those kids are being picked on in school. Because I do most of the talking during these seminars, I try to listen quietly during the breaks. I took in the conversation. What I heard was fascinating.

First, one dad said that his kid was getting beaten up at recess, behind a backstop and a snow pile, where nobody could see. The kid's mom called the principal, and the area in question was roped off the next day. Problem solved? Nope. Not surprisingly, playground scuffling is a fairly mobile activity, so the violence continued unabated. But when this dad talked more with his kid, he found out that his son was actually provoking the challenge. While he wasn't being physically aggressive, he was certainly inviting confrontation, and didn't mind the conflict or the outcome. Even though the kid was just telling stories, his parents didn't understand this and reacted.

Another mom chimed in with a very different story: her daughter was being singled out for ridicule by two specific ringleaders, who pressured other kids to stay away from her or risk ridicule. Her daughter, a top student, didn't want to go to school.

The other parents listening to these stories were very upset. One dad was out for bully-blood, angry with both schools for anemic responses. A mom disagreed: "There's nothing we can do anyway," she said. "It's kids being kids, and we are just making it worse by meddling. The bullies will win every time."

People were gathering around us. Another mom offered her story: "My son gets picked on because, well, because he is kind of nerdy. I'm trying to teach him to be cooler and to fit in better." The first dad jumped on that like a lion on a staked goat. "No!" he almost shouted. "You're blaming the victim. You just need to teach him that he's being treated unjustly, and that it isn't a reflection on him. Don't teach him to change. Teach him that he's wonderful the way he is."

Sometimes, remaining silent yields rich rewards. These responses say at least as much about their advocates as they do about the situations at hand. These days, a drive to "stop bullying" is informed, at least in part, by reported incidents where victims of chronic peer abuse have gone on to perpetrate acts of horrendous violence. Since time immemorial, parents have wanted to make life easier for their kids than it was for them. Differing perspectives on bullying can reveal broader differences in parenting styles and their underlying beliefs.

Kids can be mean – not unlike adults. Among school and youth-centered communities, we see increasing awareness of bullying and abuse and important, valuable programs to prevent them. All these parents offered wisdom, though. We want to insulate our kids from the damaging effects of bullying, and yet these challenges can offer opportunities to learn resilience and maybe new skills. Abusive behavior must be curbed, and yet we must also care for abusers – who are kids, too – helping them grow while teaching accountability for behavior.

—⁂—

Conversation Starters:
Childhood is complicated, which makes it the perfect preparation for adulthood. Bullying presents some particularly troubling complications.

- Were you a bully as a kid? Were you bullied? What did you learn from your experiences?
- What do you wish you had done differently? Was there a hidden opportunity within the bullying problem?
- How does adult bullying – and appropriate responses – differ from the childhood variety?

Ethical Intuition

December 2007

The tension between intuition and analysis can become a serious problem for leaders when either is misapplied, or when we aren't able to bring both to bear to the greatest extent possible.

When do we *just know*? This question recently arose in a meeting with a client's board of directors, presenting an organizational strategy developed with management and staff. Our recommendations were well-received, and I think well-understood. As we began to discuss implications for the strategy on project priorities, one member interrupted me. "This is way too analytical," he said. "I know a good project when I see one." He perceived a conflict and attributed it, interestingly, to "a clash of Myers-Briggs Types.[13]" When someone asked him to say more, he observed that trying to create matrices to make decisions seems at odds with intuition, with gut feel. He then went on to clarify that he wasn't denigrating intuition or analysis, just putting on the table his personal orientation toward intuition and against analy-

---

[13] The Myers-Briggs Type Indicator (MBTI) is a model for understanding personal differences that has achieved extraordinarily wide application in workplaces and even in the public consciousness. You may have participated in or overheard conversations about people's "Myers-Briggs Types," represented by four-letter categories based on the work of Carl Jung, interpreted by Isabel Briggs Myers and her mother, Katharine Briggs. I remain very cautious about efforts to describe people in terms of simple attributes, but respect that many people find meaning and insight in such systems. For more on MBTI, see www.myersbriggs.org.

sis. The grids I presented seemed meaningless to him, and so he was essentially recusing himself from the discussion at hand.

That might have been the only time that anyone has ever suggested that I was too analytical. I rely heavily on intuition as a critical faculty and as a critical factor in business success.

Malcolm Gladwell wrote a great book, entitled *Blink,* on the subject of intuition and the phenomenon of "just knowing." In it, he considers the power of intuition, and its limitations: when we ought to trust gut feel, and when we ought not. Among his key points is a strong argument that we can trust our intuitions in areas where we are genuinely experienced and knowledgeable.[14]

The tension between intuition and analysis is particularly acute where ethical decisions are concerned. Most of us have a gut feel for when something is wrong. It is easy to conclude that unethical conduct arises from ignoring our guts. There are real problems with that view of ethical reasoning, however. First, our guts – our intuitions – register a lot of inputs at once. We feel a sense of duty toward shareholders, empathy for and commitment to employees, a strong desire to please customers, etc. Second, fear can cloud moral intuition, particularly when we perceive that our livelihoods or our families' finances are at stake. So can many other emotions or circumstances that we might or might not perceive.

On the other hand, we may be able to trust our intuitions, at least to some degree, as an initial indicator of a potential problem. We may have very good gut feel for identifying when obligations or commitments are potentially in conflict, for example. We may know when something might be wrong or when something is profoundly, inexorably, undeniably wrong. However, different people have different sensitivities, different thresholds of concern, and different priorities. Individual moral intuitions are sure to vary. So, even under the best of circumstances, our ethical judgments can't be based on gut feel alone.

Analysis has its limitations as well. We come to work with different values and moral orientations. Of course, a strong set of organizational values can

---

[14] That may seem obvious, but the importance of it became clear to me when I reflected on the breadth of topics about which I have "gut feel," and the narrower subset of areas about which I actually know something. *Blink* is a quick, lively read, and I highly recommend it.

provide a good framework for discussion. Agreed-upon organizational values are a critical, perhaps necessary, but certainly insufficient basis for ethical deliberation within an organization. Even with a common framework for discussion, too many people who are adept at business analysis are unwilling or unable to engage in ethical analysis. Agreeing on common premises – then arguing through their implications to a common conclusion – is challenging. Like any skill, it takes practice. A good first step is recognizing that ethical deliberation and analysis do in fact require skill and practice.

By the same token, it is very often gut feel or intuition that alerts us to a potential problem. We ignore those intuitions at our peril. In fact, leaders should create environments where people are encouraged to speak up when they perceive a problem, and where there are processes for examining and evaluating those perceptions.

There is no single answer, no easy resolution to the tension between moral intuition and ethical reasoning or analysis. Instead, we can avoid the problems associated with that tension by first understanding the power and limits of our intuition, and then developing skills and language that enable us to communicate and evaluate ethical concerns as capably as we analyze business opportunities. Finally, we need to continue to develop shared values, frameworks, and skills for ethical deliberation within our organizations.

—ɯ—

<u>Conversation Starters:</u>
Effective decision-making is a critical skill, to be developed over a lifetime. In areas where we are genuinely knowledgeable and experienced, sometimes we can trust our intuition first and foremost.

- What kinds of decisions do you make analytically? When do you tend to act primarily from intuition?
- Can you use both, confirming intuition with further analysis, or taking a step back from deep deliberation to "check your gut" on a key decision?
- How effectively can you engage with those whose styles differ from your own?

Listen...More Carefully

October 2012

My late father used to sum up every election season the same way: "Everybody's lying, but that's okay. Nobody's listening." The more things change, the more they remain the same. Training leaders not to lie is a pointless exercise. If the importance of honesty is not obvious, what kind of training would make a difference? Excellent listening, on the other hand, is a teachable skill and, for some, a lifelong pursuit.

There is no shortage of resources and literature on listening. I have taught a number of specific techniques over the years, including appreciative and reflective listening.[15] Becoming a better listener remains a core part of any leadership development program.

About a year ago, I revamped my training segments devoted to listening. Rather than teach one set of techniques or another, I decided to work with program participants to learn about listening in part by listening to them. In one group after another, I introduced the

---

[15] I am not an expert practitioner, but I am learning more about Appreciative Inquiry, a growing area of study and practice related to organizational development and especially change management that centers on perception. Case Western Reserve University sponsors an excellent online resource collection at appreciativeinquiry.case.edu. I also value the practical listening techniques that psychologist Carl Rogers (1902-1987) called "Active Listening."

concept of listening by starting discussions about its deep power. Then I asked questions like, "What makes you feel like you are being listened to and heard?" We reflected on great listeners and effective listening techniques. We worked together to determine how we would embrace new practices and observe our progress.

The teams and audiences answering these questions have been quite varied, including cops, firefighters, nurses and allied health professionals, accountants, social workers, many groups of business managers, city workers and supervisors, and even a group of 9-year-olds. The answers, on the other hand, have been remarkably consistent. The following tips for how to be a great listener appear again and again:

Be patient; don't rush to respond. Don't finish sentences or cut someone off. Better yet, absorb what has been said before formulating your response.

Engage in discussion. Ask questions. Really respond to what you hear.

Re-state what you are hearing, and ask for clarification, especially when the topic is complex.

Recap the conversation afterward, orally or in writing.

Use body language to show you are listening. Eye contact, head nodding, open stance. Show that you are paying attention.

Take action based on the discussion. People feel listened to when their input leads to specific outcomes.

Independent of these specific words of advice, virtually every group discussion came around to the realization of how challenging good listening really is, and how easy it is to avoid listening well. Paying attention, listening with an open mind, and communicating that we are listening all require effort and, at times, discipline. The payoff for that effort is often enormous.

—ᴡ—

Conversation Starters

Good listening is hard work. It is also a set of skills worth mastering.

- If we all know how to listen well, why is there so much bad listening going on?
- What challenges do you face in listening really well?
- What ways do you find most effective to practice your listening skills?

Share your User Guide

May 2012

S ome weeks ago, my 12-year-old son got off a very funny crack about
my expanding baldness. Despite what I thought was my obvious
amusement, he quickly grew serious and asked, "Dad, did I cross the
line? Was that disrespectful? I don't want to hurt your feelings."

What he was asking for, on one level, was permission to rib me,
both retroactively and proactively. He also wanted to avoid inadver-
tently hurting my feelings. He was duly relieved by my confirmation: I
am not the least bit sensitive about my hairline (such as it is).

Below the surface was a deeper question about the ground rules
of our relationship, now that he's no longer a little kid. As our conversation continued, we considered a range of boundaries, and each
learned something about the other. He's a kind soul and a great young
man (I say this with parental bias fully acknowledged).

The discussion led me to think about times in my life when I
would have acted differently had I known more about the people
around me. I also came to realize, and to marvel at, how many times
I remembered being hurt or offended, when the person committing
the offending act or statement could not possibly have known of my
relevant sensitivities.

Charles A. Weinstein Ph.D.

We need not suffer these unintended indignities. A communication model exists that can help us. This model emerges from, of all places, the electronics equipment industry.

I recently purchased a portable audio recorder. On my own, I could figure out how to make a recording, transfer it to my PC and change a few settings. By reading the User Guide, however, I learned:

- **Hidden features**, like dual-level stereo track recording (*it's nerd-o-phonic!*).
- **Care instructions**, such as how to safely clean the microphones.
- **Cautions,** including one warning not to plug in the device while recording, lest it automatically turn itself off.

With knowledge of that sort, I was equipped to get the most out of my new purchase. Why not share analogous aspects of ourselves with our colleagues?

In my early 20s, I transitioned from a business job in Chicago to an academic job in Minneapolis. Within months, I was in hot water with my new boss, with nary a clue as to why. As we talked about her (many) frustrations with me, it became clear: my previous supervisors had taught me to greatly limit contact with them until my tasks were complete, while she expected regular updates and opportunities to provide input into my work. When we cleared that up – my "Features" and her "Cautions," if you will – we began working together fabulously.

I have been conducting a training exercise based on this idea. Participants reflect on and share those aspects of themselves that might not be obvious to their peers. In just a few weeks, we have seen some fascinating results:

- A meeting planner discovered that one of her associates had been a stand-up comedian and was able to use him when a scheduled speaker was running late.
- A CEO realized how irritated he was when people dropped in at the beginning of the day without an appointment, "before he got busy." He had never told them to make an appointment.
- An employee turned to his supervisor and asked her for more feedback, positive and negative. "No news is never good news

for me," he said, "even if you intend it to be." They agreed to change the way they worked together, and they have done so.

There are other benefits to this sharing, as well. It is easier to resolve differences with someone whom you know as a person. Much of our personhood takes place outside of work. Common interests are nice, but divergent interests are fun, too. I'm a committed omnivore, especially devoted to carnivory. I recently turned to a vegan client for an appropriate, yet interesting, recipe to bring to a recent potluck. Even that little bit of connection made it easier for us to work on some business challenges. We give one another the benefit of the doubt, without thinking about doing so. Because we know one another a bit more as people, we are able to work through conflicts more smoothly.

This kind of sharing need not be formal. You get to choose what features you share, how, and with whom. The intent is to give people the information they need to work with you, in ways that are mutually satisfying. What could be bad?

—∿—

Conversation Starters

Let the people around you know what makes you tick, and get to know them as people as you allow them to know you.

- Share your user guide with others! Start with your passions outside of work, and then progress to your work styles and preferences.
- Provide feedback to others, as well: let them know when you are surprised by what you learned from their sharing.
- What is something surprising that you have learned about someone with whom you work, and how did it contribute to your work together?

Embracing Gravity and Friction, on and off the Slopes

March 2008

A few weeks ago, I had a most enjoyable day skiing in northern Minnesota. For those familiar with skiing in the Midwest, it typically involves very short runs into a river valley or, in this case, down from the bluffs surrounding Lake Superior. Some of the runs have names like "Wendell's Widowmaker," but nobody really believes them. It was a beautiful, sunny day, I was with a dear friend, and we had a great time.

During the many (many, many) trips up the chair lift, I got to thinking. I began to reflect on the physics of skiing, a topic of pressing interest given my recent lapses in strength training. In our daily lives, gravity and friction are physical forces that we usually view as slowing us down. We use gasoline or jet fuel to overcome these forces in order to get where we want to go. Our business metaphors imagine us "achieving lift-off" to overcome gravity or "streamlining" to reduce drag and friction. We see these forces as the enemies of progress. Without gravity and friction, however, skiing turns into, well, either standing or falling.

On the ski slope, gravity and friction are our friends, so long as we treat them as such. Gravity gives us speed. Friction, when channeled into the edges of our skis, gives us control. We manage these forces to propel us down the hill and away from rocks, trees, and other skiers. When those forces manage us, we find ourselves carving snow with our noses rather than our edges.

The connection to business seemed clear. Do we manage the forces that drive our business, or do they manage us? More accurately, do we manage our business in harmony with those forces, or in opposition to them? Do we see vendors and customers as partners in efficient, mutually beneficial transactions, or do we seek the upper hand in these relationships at every opportunity? Are competitors enemies to be crushed, or do we seek to benefit from them when we can? Great competitors can help us expand markets, drive demand, and even promote innovation.

On the ski slope, the sensations of harmony and disharmony are unmistakable. Skiing *with* the mountain is smooth, flowing, gentle. We look downhill and flow from turn to turn, aware of our surroundings as a gestalt, making decisions and acting on them in a continuous process. Skiing *against* the mountain is a different experience altogether. It may begin with anxiety or inattention, and quickly devolve into a series of disconnected moves calculated, however desperately, to keep us upright. We perceive a series of snapshots and try to react accordingly. All too often, the result is both sudden and sodden.

In our work lives, disharmony may be harder to perceive, until we are dangerously in its cold embrace. Many of our performance measures are actually following indicators. The forces that ultimately result in reduced performance may have been operating for some time before the results show up in measurable performance indicators. Mild employee discontent may go unnoticed until key people start to leave; customers' needs or preferences change and they tolerate a mild mismatch with our services until...they don't. Key vendors experience problems that we are unaware of until we find ourselves without the products we need to do our jobs.

A great strategy for preventing these kinds of operational spills involves cultivating strong, trusting relationships with the people who touch our organizations. That way we can perceive problems as they emerge and move smoothly toward their resolution before they become disruptive. It's another good reason for understanding those relationships while you are in the flow of successful work, and investing in maintaining that flow.

—⚏—

Conversation Starters

Sometimes weaknesses are also strengths, and challenges are primarily opportunities. Learn to appreciate balance, and practice looking at situations from differing perspectives.

- Do you know what it feels like to be "in the flow?" Can you sense when your team or organization is skiing with the hill, and when it is beginning to ski against it?
- If you have many years of experience, how has your ability to perceive when you are out of balance changed over the course of your career?
- What are some of your tips for correcting course, and for finding and cultivating relationships that flow?

Part III

In the Public Square

Western Philosophy has its roots in the public square. Quite literally, the ancient Greeks practiced philosophy in public, on porches (or *stoa,* from which we get the term, "stoicism") and in the marketplace (the *agora,* which created good reasons to become agora-phobic). While the practice of moral philosophy has moved indoors for the most part, public life remains a primary topic of interest.

Our contemporary democratic principles arose from the work of philosophers both ancient and modern: from Plato and Aristotle; from Hobbes, Locke, and Rousseau, who considered what makes a just government; from Kant and Bentham and the Mills;[16] and even from contemporary philosophers who seek to inform those who govern and lead the institutions that define our contemporary, public lives. It is worth noting that other philosophical traditions around the world also gave rise to systems of government, from Native American tribes and communities to the Confucian-inspired governmental systems of China. In all these instances, philosophical words informed public action. It is right, therefore, that some of our reflections address the best ways to function in the public, including political, realm.

---

[16] John Stuart Mill, and his life and writing partner Harriet Mill. They reached the unfortunate (if not unreasonable) conclusion that acknowledging her co-authorship would have threatened the credibility of the work in those sexist times. They did the Utilitarian thing, pursuing what they took to be an optimized outcome in light of the power of their ideas. John Stuart also wrote passionately and persuasively on the equality of women.

At Ethical Leaders in Action, more than half of our work is with public safety agencies. These police, fire, and emergency medical service (EMS) organizations are typically led by appointed chief officers and governed, ultimately, by elected officials. In general, there is great value in sharing learning across contexts. A director of nursing in a nursing home might have practices for motivating nursing assistants that would also work for a fire chief, while the chief's practices in emergency response might help a nursing staff maintain safe service levels through a blizzard or other crisis. At the same time, there are distinctive features of leadership in public agencies, and in the broader political and governmental context. This section includes essays that consider ethical leadership as it pertains to government and public institutions.

Taking the Pledge

"I pledge Allegiance to the Flag of the United States of America, and to the Republic for which it stands...."

May 2010

To take the Pledge of Allegiance is a remarkable act, although what is remarkable about it is too often overlooked.

The first pledge, composed by Francis Bellamy in 1892, was deliberately simple and brief: *"I pledge allegiance to my flag and the republic for which it stands: one nation indivisible with liberty and justice for all."* It has been expanded, if not necessarily improved, at several points since then.[17]

A pledge is not just a statement, but a speech act, committing the speaker to...something. To what do we commit when we "pledge allegiance?" Certainly that pledge implies a promise to refrain from treason or sedition, so espionage and terrorism are out. If that were all, we would be wasting a great deal of time, in schools and in Congress, pledging simply to avoid what is prohibited by law and in some instances punishable by death. There must be more.

---

[17] Thanks to *Wikipedia* for the text and for a fascinating account of the Pledge's history.

Indeed, the Pledge might mean much more, particularly in our current political climate. First, the Pledge offers common ground. One might quibble with a word or phrase, but we can agree to pledge allegiance to the Republic, can't we? We all benefit from a public committed to principles of liberty and justice. On that basis, all elected officials and political participants have much more in common than the current level of hostility would suggest.

Second, if we are truly serious about allegiance to the Republic, then we must also agree to act in ways that serve it. That means creating and promoting public policies that are just and truly good for the public. It also means refraining from speech and actions that imperil effective policy making. Lying, in all of its varied forms, cannot contribute to truly good government. Allowing venom (or sheer idiocy) to displace constructive dialog does not advance our understanding of complex issues or promote effective decision making. Too much contemporary speech obscures rather than reveals the truth. One poignant example: if we are serious about our own patriotism, then we ought to be very, very cautious about impugning another's, even when we disagree vehemently. Hostile political rhetoric is not mere noise. Lies and invective harm the processes, and impugn the civic values, on which the Republic depends.

Finally, while the Pledge is most frequently recited by schoolchildren, those who engage in governance of the Republic must agree to act more like adults, much more of the time. It starts with all of us.

—⁂—

Conversation Starters
Let us commit to seek truth, protect liberty, and pursue justice in our public discourse. Engaging in civil and constructive dialog is an act of patriotism.
- Where does advocacy of a position give way to damaging the processes of good governance?

- If one side stoops to empty rhetoric, how can another maintain the high ground without losing in an otherwise substantive policy dispute?
- If we agree that political speech has become harmful to good policy-making, how can we step back from that brink?

Leadership Values for Public Service

April 2011

Tough economic times prompt tough debates about the role of government and the efficacy of public institutions and employees. Constructive debate is grounded in reason as it seeks to address tough problems. Good discourse sheds light and informs wise action.

Too often, though, our public discourse generates much more heat than light. Criticism of public employees can be especially vicious, and therefore especially unhelpful. I work with leaders in public safety – fire, emergency medical service (EMS), and law enforcement – and I see great people providing excellent service, every day. I believe that public leaders need better tools for leading this discussion toward rational assessment of how public work is done and supported in our communities.

I have been working within several public safety leadership development programs to develop a framework of values that can guide leaders and inform public discourse:

1. **Excellent public service.** Do excellent work, consistent with the public's needs. Respond to, and thoughtfully inform, the public's priorities for public service.
2. **Sound stewardship of resources.** Use public funds responsibly and intelligently, in pursuit of excellent service. Make

purchases that aim for sufficiency and consider total cost of ownership. Conserve resources.

3. **Fairness.** Treat employees fairly, consistent with high expectations of service and stewardship. Articulate and apply principles of fairness across all stakeholders. Share information openly, as appropriate.

While it remains a work in progress, this framework is strong enough to build upon, and capable of informing and improving our public discourse. It has been tested and honed in more than 200 focus groups, working sessions, and training programs; for about two years, we have used the value set as a training and consulting tool while actively soliciting feedback and improving the framework itself.

These three values stand in constructive tension with one another. Public leaders should strive for excellence, with clear missions and dedicated execution. At the same time, leaders must be cautious about expenditures, assuring that the right priorities are efficiently pursued. Fair practices surely include safety, reasonable compensation and clear performance expectations. In this context, our conception of fairness must also include accountability for both service and stewardship.

Putting these values into action requires robust discussion. What is excellent service? What should the public fund and what should we expect from that funding? Stewardship demands that expenditures be linked to performance. More money must buy more or better services. Finally, agencies and communities must define the principles of fairness under which they will operate. Ultimately, fair practices lead to good performance.

These values form a basis for challenging mediocrity and waste; they also enable leaders to recognize excellence and efficiency. Rather than resorting to empty criticism and mutual mistrust, perhaps those engaged in discourse on the boundaries and nature of public service can use this value framework to find common ground. From a shared set of values, we can rationally evaluate and improve the work of government in ways that benefit us all.

—⟋⟍—

Conversation Starters

Public sector leaders can use these three values to make decisions and to frame constructive discussions with stakeholders.

- What is the role of the public sector labor unions in advancing these three values? Can labor and management work together to set and uphold high standards for service, and to provide a fair working environment, at a reasonable cost to the public?
- If you are a leader in the public sector, can you apply these values to decisions you make? Can you participate in good-faith discussions about appropriate service and spending levels?
- If you are a leader in a public agency, how do your organizational values compare with this value set?

The Madoff Decade: Far Too Simple

New Year's Day, 2010

I have always been deeply **skeptical of attempts to simplify and summarize complex phenomena. In particular, I am skeptical of reporters' desires, at the turn of decades, to summarize the decade that passed in** 500 words or 90 seconds.[18]

I am more than skeptical of a current trend, represented by one broadcaster's characterization of the past 10 years as, **"the Madoff Decade."** When I first heard that phrase on the radio, I almost swerved off the road. First, scumbaggery, even epic scumbaggery, is nothing new. Swindling, corruption and abuses are as old as humanity. Further, criminals didn't drive the current crisis, they merely punctuated it. While a great deal of value recently disappeared, the vast majority of losses were due to actions that were legal. *It wasn't, for example, criminal to propose to homeowners, "When the interest rate on this loan jumps, you can just refinance! Real estate values always go up...."* Much suffering has resulted from actual crimes by Madoff and others, but to focus too narrowly on that malfeasance is to miss the lessons we might otherwise learn from our mistakes.

---

[18] As noted above, this essay first appeared on New Year's Day, 2010. I am aware of the argument that the decade actually began in 2011, but I don't really care that much. I don't think you should, either.

Charles A. Weinstein Ph.D.

Most important, these events ought not define our lives, nor even a period of time. I recently spoke at a Rotary Club regional leadership program.[19] Multiple questions referred to "the abysmal state of ethics in this country." I'm not buying that premise. In ethical terms, recent transgressions pale in comparison to longstanding wrongs like slavery and institutionalized racism. Even in strictly economic terms, it is worth noting that the recent crisis was most painful precisely because so many people are now invested in the economy as shareholders, and not solely as wage-earners.

The exploitation of workers, while still present and always deplorable, is not business as usual, which was the case just a couple of generations ago. While we struggle with climate change today, 30 years ago it was hazardous to even touch the waters of the Potomac, the Schuylkill, or the Hudson rivers at some landings. To characterize a decade in terms of a thief, or even an economic downturn, is to negate the progress that we have made.

This isn't an idle matter of historical accuracy. If we believe that we are in the midst of moral decay, we are naturally inclined to act accordingly. We feel invited to lower our standards, and inhibited from trusting, even where trust is appropriate. I spend my days working with ethical leaders in business, health care, and public safety. I am consistently inspired by their stories, and know that they represent just the smallest sampling of excellence that exists in our business and civic communities. If we become obsessed with those who do wrong, we fail to learn from the true leaders among us.

—m—

---

[19] I am not a Rotarian, but I am impressed by the work of this international service organization, and have met many remarkable leaders as I have been welcomed to present my perspective on ethical leadership at local and regional Rotary Club meetings. www.rotary.org.

Conversation Starters

We cannot let the worst of us define an era, or frame our perspective on society. There are so many examples of great leaders from whom we can learn and draw inspiration.

- Are there leaders you admire? What aspects of their character do you seek to cultivate in yourself?
- What actions or public movements inspire you?
- What causes or purposes have moved you in the past? What has changed since that time? What are your newer passions, and why?

Asking the Right Questions about Public Employees

February 2011

As government budgets occupy the political consciousness, rhetoric about public employees is heating up. Some pundits advocate outsourcing public work or reforming public employment, while others argue the public employees actually represent a good value, in part because they may be paid less than private counterparts for some kinds of work. At a deeper level, we all agree: we want public employees to provide excellent quality and value. Then we can decide what functions and services are appropriately filled by public agencies.

There are no magic solutions. If we agree that our goal is efficient and excellent public service, we can work together to solve the problems and eliminate the barriers to that objective. Achieving that goal should be no harder – but it will also be no easier – than it is in the private sector. Have you ever had bad service from a private sector employer? Ever ordered a hamburger (or an angiogram, for that matter) and been disappointed by the experience? Of course. We don't jump to the conclusion that the employees involved were pampered or overpaid.

My perspective on this issue is informed by my work as a consultant and trainer in the public sector; I teach and develop ethical leadership in law enforcement and fire/EMS organizations. Every day I see great people committed to doing excellent work. Do I encounter a few grumblers or knuckleheads? Yes, a few. Such is the human condition. However, my experience overwhelmingly involves workers that any employer would be proud to employ. There are certainly problems and challenges in public organizations, but I have seen nothing to justify the level of angst that I hear from some elected officials and many media pundits.

Raising public ire will not improve productivity. Leadership might, if it begins with clearly articulated objectives, and translates them into observable outcomes and measures. Leadership could then get the right people into the right roles, set expectations, and provide appropriate support so that public employees can effectively serve the public. Compensation plans must enable public employers to attract and retain the right workers. Management must promote worker engagement and effective pursuit of well-defined missions. The workers, in turn, must be held accountable for the outcomes that best serve the public.

I do not believe that public employees should be above criticism, but that criticism must be aimed at constructive solutions. The debate should focus on driving actual improvements, rather than bemoaning the *status quo* or throwing in the towel. When we roll up our sleeves and strive for excellence, we make great progress. I see public employees doing just that, almost every day. (And, for the record, who doesn't have bad days once in a while?)

—∿—

Conversation Starters
Public employees should be led well: held to high standards in pursuit of clear missions, and recognized for good work. They also deserve fair treatment in our public discourse about the proper scope of government.

- What should the government do? At what level of government?
- What criteria are you using to make those choices?
- Can you see the logic that might lead others to reach different conclusions?

Leading with Lunch

November 2012

This week I had a great lunch with my friend David, who was hired as a manager to drive change in a well-established organization. As an experienced leader, David could see the organization's strengths, shortcomings, and idiosyncrasies with fresh eyes. Mostly, he saw interpersonal conflicts. Some of these conflicts are new and fresh, some old and stale, and some are ancient and festering. This is David's honeymoon: nobody resents him. He is using this magic time to forge new relationships and to prepare his team to pursue new strategies.

I asked about his strategic priorities. The answer surprised me. "Our strategic priorities are less important than operations at the moment; I'm very hands-on right now," David said. "A lot of times, I'm doing what we're doing here, having lunch." These aren't working lunches, either. They are for getting acquainted, for connecting and relaxing together in the midst of hectic work days.

It is easy to forget how powerful a casual lunch can be, in establishing (or repairing) relationships. We sit down, we face one another and we talk. We eat, we relax, we enjoy a meal in one another's company, and before we know it, we are enjoying one another's company. At the very least, we are learning more about the people with whom we work and allowing them to know us better. How can that not help us later on, as we work together to solve problems or to pursue our common objectives?

David sees changes already. When he mentioned that a technician was coming in to repair some equipment, one of his team members was surprised. "We've been asking them to work on that for months and months," she said. "How did you do it?"

"We had lunch a few weeks ago, so it was easy to call and ask for their help."

What else is possible?

Gazillions of dollars have been spent across the nation to convince voters that one candidate or another is incompetent, ill-intentioned, somehow dangerous, or just plain scuzzy. If I had a little of that money back, I'd spend it differently: on pizzas and sandwiches. I'd buy lunches for the people who have been elected, and for those who will be appointed, to public office. I would invite them to get to know one another as people. They need to connect across party lines as adults, and to acknowledge their common objectives before they start hammering on their differences. When old-timers reflect on more civil times, they always tell the same story, of cocktail hours and dinners over which political rivals could relax and find common ground.

This isn't just true of officials, either. They function as part of a system that includes political parties, interest groups, advocates, media organizations, and voters. We are all, collectively and in different ways, responsible for public policy and governance. As participants in public leadership, we generally need to grow up, come together when we can, and then reach thoughtful compromises and wise decisions on the issues that remain.

What better way to start than over lunch?

—⟊⟊—

Conversation Starters:
The public would be well-served if political adversaries could show respect for one another. A meal is a good context for the kinds of civil conversations that build respectful relationships.
- Would you consider reaching out to an adversary to try to make a connection over lunch?

- How would you respond if an adversary reached out to you?
- What are the barriers to civil and constructive discourse among elected officials?
- What kind of leadership will be required to break them down?

A Little Less Fear and Loathing

November 2010

When I was growing up in Saint Louis Park, Minnesota, *Star Wars* was playing at the Cooper Theater. Forever. It was the perfect venue for that film, featuring a huge screen and great audio combined with spacious surroundings, even a smoking lounge. It was a place of great, retro class. Today that land is occupied by a brand-new, snazzy mixed use development. There is a bar named for the old theater.

Star Wars lives on, a media juggernaut that includes some now-old-fashioned DVDs. We're watching them now, in order of release. My kids had not yet seen them, and we're all enjoying them a great deal. On one level, the series stands as a history of late 20th century special effects. At a deeper level, I am taking curious comfort in the story: good and evil are clearly delineated. In a fantasy world, long ago and far away, Evil wore predictable costumes and was audibly enrobed in recognizable musical themes.

The real world is much more complicated, of course – unless you believe the political ads that mercifully ended with yesterday's election. These ads depicted monsters and madmen, all bent on destroying civilization as we know it. The tenor, and often the content, of our political rhetoric have transcended even Star Wars melodrama.

Unlike the movies, this isn't good, clean fun. Venom and lies obscure reality and prevent leaders from making sound policy decisions. This talk scares me.

I see no signs of change, so I'm done looking for it around me. Instead, I commit to change myself. Beginning now, I will listen to those with whom I disagree, seeking truth and wisdom in their statements. I will look to improve my perspectives and opinions by listening to theirs. Absent compelling evidence to the contrary, I will assume that those with whom I disagree still want to implement the right policies for the right reasons.

A note of caution and clarification is in order. Some ideas are wrong, even harmful. Some people are ill-intentioned, even bad. I am not advocating stepping back from critical thinking or suspending our values or principles. Rather, I am arguing that we can still think critically and stand up for our beliefs while we open our minds and engage respectfully, even with adversaries.

These ideas are not new, and they are not mine alone. Stephen Covey's *Seven Habits* include seeking to understand before we seek to be understood. We'll see if I can practice this habit without my head exploding.

—⦿—

Conversation Starters
In life, unlike the movies, there are few instances of true black and white, and many more shades of grey. Listening carefully and interpreting charitably what we hear can do a long way toward better policymaking, better business, and better leadership overall.
- Do you tend to cast someone with whom you disagree as Darth Vader?
- Can you remain open and listen to opposing viewpoints?
- Can we begin to expect that level of maturity of public officials, as well?

Learning the Right Lessons

September 11, 2011

I spent the afternoon of September 11, 2011 remembering September 11, 2001, when I was in the company of thousands attending the "Minnesota Remembers" program in Eden Prairie, Minnesota. Dignitaries and public servants spoke about the courage and service of our community's first responders. Fire service, emergency medical service, and law enforcement leaders spoke with passion and clarity about the excellence of their people and the need for continued public support. All who gathered remembered and reflected, together. It was an excellent program, thoughtfully planned and poignantly executed. I was moved.

As we reflected on our past, I was struck by thoughts for our future. First, let it not go without saying that the people who help us to be safe, and who aid us when we are in trouble, are worthy of our respect, gratitude, and support. By virtue of their efforts, we have become safer in the last 10 years: fortifying, becoming more vigilant, imagining and deterring future threats. We have invested to prevent and to prepare for violent acts, which a decade ago seemed too remote to warrant that investment. Our work is not done.

Second, the events of 9/11 and its aftermath reflect both the darkest and the brightest aspects of humanity. As Pastor Dan Carlson reminded us in his brilliant (and, I was grateful to note, truly non-denominational) benediction, no group has a monopoly on either darkness or the light.[20] We are all capable of kindness as well as cruelty, of ennobling wisdom as well as dangerous foolishness. We can connect, and we can alienate. The defining moments we commemorate reveal much about our very humanity; we are at once strong and vulnerable.

Our vulnerabilities encompass not only physical violence but moral risk, as well. In the days following the atrocity, many pundits opined that we were attacked precisely because our nation is a bastion of freedom and tolerance. I have come to believe that our future must include greater efforts to understand one another in ways that diminish the hatred and alienation that motivate such attacks.

We must also commit to defend our values along with our safety. Too often in our responses, we have weakened the very values which we purport to defend. We have been less than judicious in protecting privacy and liberty in the face of remote or imagined threats. We have also stooped to xenophobia. According to *The New York Times*, in the past year more than two dozen states have considered laws preventing judges from consulting Islamic law in deciding cases. Is this really a pressing threat to jurisprudence, or a jingoistic red herring? I attended a conference last year where a vendor sold t-shirts stating, "Everything I need to know about Islam I learned on 9/11." Conference organizers compelled him to stop selling the unauthorized merchandise, but what of the buyers? We have much work to do.

Let us spend the next decade improving how we protect and express the values that have made ours a great nation. Let us seek to connect across barriers, with the same creativity and zeal with which we erect protective barriers. Let us remember our vulnerability, our strength, our character, and our humanity.

—〰—

---

[20] Dan Carlson is a retired police chief and ordained Lutheran minister who has become an influential leader in public safety chaplaincy. I am also grateful to consider him a friend.

Conversation Starters

There are no monopolies on darkness or light. Especially where public policy is concerned, beware of seeking simplicity at the expense of truth; be willing to accept complexity and ambiguity.

- We often find conversations such as these challenging because we are required to hold beliefs that are in tension with one another. For example, do you agree with both of the following propositions:
    1. The violence of 9/11 is inexcusable and the perpetrators should be found and punished.
    2. The violence of 9/11 was caused, in part, by hatred that could be mitigated through better understanding between cultures.
- How would you change either of the foregoing statements to better reflect your beliefs? Are your beliefs still in tension?
- Where would you draw the line with respect to abridging rights in the name of security? Why?

Disarming Conversation

November 2010

My home phone rang Wednesday night; the same Arizona number had called several times before. This time I answered, and acknowledged that I was indeed Charles Weinstein.

"Mr. Weinstein, I'm Robert Alvarez, and I'm calling for the National Rifle Association."[21]

Oy vey.

I own guns, and I hunt. My purchases of firearms and hunting licenses place me on some interesting lists.

The caller asked about my current season, and (oddly) we commiserated that work and life demands had kept each of us from the fields so far this year. Then Mr. Alvarez turned to his business, describing recent gun control recommendations made by a United Nations Commission, and explaining that President Obama supported these recommendations. The National Rifle Association (NRA), it seemed, needed my support (presumably moral, but certainly financial).

---

[21] The caller's name is changed, but he did in fact represent the NRA.

I explained that I am actually in favor of some gun control measures, and that I would abide by appropriate restrictions, if they could reasonably be expected to create a safer society.

"Well, we disagree," he said. "I believe that the right to bear arms should not be abridged, and that it is a cornerstone of a safe society. Thank you for speaking with me tonight. Have a Happy Thanksgiving."

I extended the same wishes to him, sincerely. We need more discourse like this.

This representative of the NRA was pleasant, reasonable, respectful, and articulate. He referred to the President as such, without audible derision. Our policy disagreement did not require either of us to be nasty. This is precisely the constructive spirit we need to address social problems large and small, and to maintain (or, one might argue, to create) a functioning Republic.

Civility is effective. That brief conversation led me to think more critically about my willingness to curtail a constitutional protection. A broader right to privacy is likewise challenged by increasingly explicit scanning technologies deployed to our airports. Should flying constitute "implied consent," as driving an automobile implies consent to a breath or blood test? What is the nature of the right to privacy? Does the risk of terrorism justify the curtailment of that right? These are important questions, and Mr. Alvarez of the NRA was effective at raising them.

—∽—

Conversation Starters
Civility works.
- Do you respond differently if someone you disagree with speaks reasonably and respectfully?
- Does this type of approach to an argument keep your mind more open to listen to all points of view?
- What do we gain as a society when such conversations increase our openness and attentiveness to different points of view, even if people are not persuaded to change their opinions and allegiances?

Picking Our Heroes

February 2009

Every time a prominent athlete is caught misbehaving, people respond to my presentations and blog posts, in part, by asking my opinions of the misbehavior. So, when the news broke that Olympic champion Michael Phelps was photographed smoking marijuana, the question was inevitable: *"What do you think about Michael Phelps?"*[22]

I think he swims really, really fast. Shockingly, consistently, record-breakingly fast. I think he's an unusual looking fellow. Oh, and I read somewhere that in 2008 he was photographed while smoking marijuana, and in 2004 pled guilty to driving while intoxicated. He apologized, fairly convincingly, both times. He appears to be accepting the consequences of his actions with class.

Some aspects of the Michael Phelps discussion are clear-cut and obvious. First, driving while intoxicated is both illegal and morally wrong. It puts innocent people at risk. Second, it was unforgivably scuzzy of a fellow partier to photograph Phelps with the bong and to sell those photos to the news media. Third, if Phelps's agents really tried to buy off the photographers, then that might seem scuzzy too. I'd need to think more about that.

---

[22] Michael Phelps was, according to his Web page, "the most decorated Olympian of all times," with 22 medals. This essay could have been about any number of celebrities, at any time (e.g., Lindsay Lohan, Tiger Woods, etc.). If you don't remember Michael Phelps, then this book has, happily, stood the test of time.

Charles A. Weinstein Ph.D.

Some ethicist I turn out to be.

The morality of pot smoking is complex. Smoking marijuana was illegal when Phelps did it, though laws are changing in many places. We might liken it to the morality of drinking during Prohibition. It was against the law, and it was at odds with his personal "brand" as an athlete, and presumably with the values of some of his sponsors.

Phelps said he was sorry, that he made a mistake. That is honorable, as far as it goes. It is certainly more honorable than either Bill Clinton's infamous, "I didn't inhale," or George W. Bush's blanket refusal to confirm or deny any drug use before age 28, but those responses set extremely low bars.

Phelps isn't running for leader of the free world. Instead, he's swimming really fast. He has signed celebrity endorsement contracts, and will lose at least some of them as a result of the photos. That brings to the fore the most interesting aspect of the situation: why are people disappointed by his actions?

I understand, to some degree, why sponsors such as Kellogg's might drop Phelps. Nobody wants to encourage kids to use drugs, and Kellogg's presumably paid Phelps, at least in part, to encourage them to eat breakfast cereals (we might consider the ethical dimensions of Froot Loops™ some other time). His conduct might also seem to complicate Kellogg's fitness-oriented brand claims, though it may be hard to argue that whatever was in that pipe slowed him down much.

Why is his endorsement valuable in the first place? Because we project onto celebrities all sorts of fanciful qualities, and want them to reflect those qualities. We are then shocked and disappointed when they fail to live up to our baseless expectations. All we know about Phelps is that he swims fast. If we are seeking the endorsement of an expert in swimming fast, he's our guy. If we hold him up as more than a fast swimmer, we are engaged in a flight of fancy.

—ᴡ—

Conversation Starters:

Let us not confuse celebrity with heroism. Let us pick our heroes carefully.

- Do you idolize celebrities?
- Whom would you make a celebrity, if you could, and why?
- Who are your heroes?

Dedication

October 2012[23]

"If you need a bottle of water, please raise your hand and an usher will bring one to you."

I was seated among thousands gathered to witness – no, to participate in – the dedication of the Minnesota Fallen Firefighter Memorial. We had walked past the aerial truck arches, heard the bell toll in memory of Minnesota's 207 firefighters lost in the line of duty, and observed as an honor guard advanced the colors to the cadence of a pipe and drum corps.

Before the day was over, we would be moved by thoughtful speeches. We would learn about the memorial's symbols, wrought of steel and stone. We would witness an apparently endless column of firefighters, advancing slowly with flags and roses to be presented to the families of the fallen. I have never heard so many people remain so silent, so still, for so long. It was the most respectful space in which I have ever been present. The solemnity continued with a bell ceremony, before the mood was gently lifted by the release of doves. The white birds circled in the still air, then departed for destinations unknown to us.

The firefighters and officers with whom I work each day as a consultant and trainer showed their very best that day. At the same time,

---

[23] This essay first appeared in a book given to families honored at the dedication. It was my privilege to have made small contribution to the creation and dedication of this striking memorial.

they remained authentic. Their salutes were clearly practiced, their brass was polished, but their warm smiles and the tears in many eyes were every bit their own. The atmosphere was welcoming and open, the language inclusive and appreciative of all who came to participate in this dedication. It was a day of great beauty and deep meaning.

Still, it was in a seemingly small detail – the provision of water for all guests – that I saw so much of what is truly great about the fire service. The planners and participants were prepared. They were thoughtful, and they were kind. Crisply uniformed firefighters and officers offered water to everyone, meeting guests' needs and attending to their comfort in a way that preserved the dignity of the moment. The water was cold, while the caring welcome it represented was very warm.

Today we have a memorial, rich with symbolism, dedicated by the extended community. I plan to visit and linger there, remembering, reflecting, and honoring all that is great about the fire service. Surely that includes those mercifully rare acts of supreme sacrifice memorialized in steel, but just as surely I will appreciate the daily acts of service, competence, and kindness performed by the members of each department named in stone.

—⟪⟫—

Conversation Starters:
Public ceremonies are important. Let us celebrate not just physical courage, but compassion and service, as well.
- Do you take time for ceremony? What rituals move you?
- Do you feel a part of the traditions of your profession, or your "tribe?" Does that have an effect on how you conduct your business or other aspects of your life, and why?
- What place do public gathering and rituals have in our modern, often "virtual" business world?

Part IV

In the Workplace: Relationships and

Organizations

For nearly everyone, leading a meaningful and healthy life involves connections with others. That is how life gets complicated. Very often, those connections exist within broader social or organizational structures. Ethicists tend to perk up at the mention of relationships and organizations, eager as we are to generate rules and systems for preventing wrongdoing. Perhaps the greatest contemporary movement in business ethics, the rise of stakeholder thinking, first recognized that business relationships are interconnected and immediately began to articulate the ethical obligations implied by those complex connections. Public safety ethics likewise focuses on duties, preventing abuses of power and seeking to maintain the public trust. It is nearly impossible to discuss law enforcement ethics without immediately turning to potential abuses of power and authority. When I began teaching ethics in the fire service, people asked, "Why? What do firefighters do that is unethical?"

But wait! Why do we continue to think of ethics only in terms of minimal expectations?

What would happen if we focused not on our obligations and duties, nor on ethical violations, but on the remarkable opportunities to make a positive difference in the world? Certainly, there are moral duties to which we ought to attend, but if we stop with our duties, we miss the richness in life that ethical leadership can bring to us. In relationships with others, we find the opportunities to be our best as human beings. In organizations, we find structures that enable us to expand our efforts and to pursue greatness.

The essays in this section focus on the same positive perspective on ethics that we have been exploring thus far, set in the varied context of workplaces. Most of these essays apply the concepts that have been introduced so far – like the merits of exceeding minimal expectations and the power of building strong, trust-based relationships – to specific functions, like building vendor relationships or conducting performance reviews. We also present a few new skills and ideas for your consideration. The overall aim is to stimulate your thinking about how to use the concepts of ethical leadership in your daily work life.

Mother's Day

May 2009

On Mother's Day I think it fitting to reflect on a couple of the lessons I learned from my late mother, Adrienne Weinstein, on the topic of ethical leadership. Before I do, I must also share a more general, personal reflection on parenting itself.

As a child, I had no idea how incredible it was to have meals prepared for me and laundry done, to say nothing of the basics of shelter, clothing, and especially love. I thought I was grateful. Looking back from the perspective of a parent, I can safely say that I had no foggy idea how challenging it really was, simply to put reasonably nutritious and tasty food on the table, one meal after another. I now understand why my father said, "People who show up and do what is expected of them – do their work, pay their bills, take care of their family – are minor heroes."

Adrienne didn't regard herself as a hero, minor or otherwise. She used to joke that her epitaph was to read, "She tried." (Come to think of it, that desire may have reflected some transitory frustration regarding one or both of her sons. Moving right along….) In fact, she did far better than try. Adrienne had a career in retail advertising, culminating in over 20 years with a Minneapolis retailer,[24] ultimately as director of cor-

---

[24] That firm was Bachman's, a regional retailer. They were profoundly supportive of my mother through her illness at the end of her life, which I will forever admire and appreciate.

porate communications. She evolved into that role as I was moving into the business world myself, so we had a great deal to talk about. Much of what I know about ethical leadership came from those discussions.

Adrienne knew as much about building relationships as anyone I have ever met. I have used assessment tools to help clients evaluate the ethical soundness of their key business relationships. As good as they were, I could never have sold those tools to my own mother. She had her own process: She became friends with many of the people she did business with, and then continued to treat them like friends unless there was a compelling, overwhelming reason to do otherwise. I'm not talking about friendly associates here. I'm talking about friends. Mutually concerned, mutually trusting, mutually supportive friends. It was uncanny.

This was not a strategy, but an expression of who Adrienne was. Authenticity is a somewhat hot concept now, but she exhibited it long before anyone named it. At various points in her career, she learned some techniques for modulating her candor and openness as appropriate – crying when you are angry can be problematic in a business setting, so she adapted accordingly – but the remarkable lesson was that she was able to fully be herself at work, and that led her to form very strong relationships, with vendors, partners and colleagues. She truly loved her company, and ultimately her coworkers loved her, too.

In particular, turning vendors into "frienders" has its benefits and its risks, which we debated at length. She pointed out all the times that people went out of their way to deliver excellent service because of the strength of their relationship with her, and I argued that she left herself vulnerable by trusting vendors so fully. In truth, the debate didn't matter, because Adrienne was just being Adrienne. In rare instances when a vendor – a friend – disappointed her, she was in fact deeply disappointed and hurt. When they did great, she felt gratitude and cheered them along with equal passion and enthusiasm. Mostly, they did great.

As I got older, I also realized the degree to which Adrienne was making choices, albeit choices consistent with her nature. She knew when not to trust, and when to "trust and verify." She made mistakes but believed that the cost of those few mistakes was tiny compared to the benefits of rich, enduring business relationships. For her, doing business this way was not only good business, but an important dimension of making her work meaningful and giving it her all.

—ɷ—

Conversation Starters:
Strong, trust-based relationships offer real business benefits. They also entail personal and commercial risks.

- Do you build strong relationships with vendors or other partners? What makes them strong relationships?
- What are the barriers to building those relationships? Do you fear being taken advantage of? Do you feel inclined to trust others?
- Does the way you operate in business reflect the way you grew up and the example your parents set?

With a Little Help from my Friends

August 2010

About three years ago, I was invited to meet with an organization with a very common complaint: "We don't work well together." This was a small company, and everyone seemed highly competent and engaged in their work. People got along. I looked for deep, simmering conflicts, and found none. Yet, too often, people worked alone when they should have worked together. They tended to wing it, even when relevant skills and experience could be found in the same room. Not surprisingly, there were consequences. Deadlines were missed, budgets were blown, and customers were frustrated.

After many interviews and much discussion, I discovered the root of the problem: nobody asked for help.

That case stands out in my mind because it existed in an otherwise happy, healthy workplace, but this "excessive individualism" is pretty common. If we take a moment to reflect – on other's behavior, never our own! – this becomes quite clear.

Executive coach Tom Laughlin puts it this way: "The primary model that we use in building community is based not on people's willingness to *give* help, but on their willingness to *ask* for help."[25] In fact, there are generally many more people willing to help than to ask

---

[25] Tom Laughlin is a member of Ethical Leaders in Action, president of his own firm, Caravela, Inc., and a friend and mentor. His practical insights into the nature of teams and communities have informed my work for years.

for it. At the very core of community is a shared willingness to support one another. That means that community members must also be willing to be supported.

Let's admit that asking for help seems risky. We feel like we understand our own capabilities and motives, but we may question those of others. Asking for help can also make us vulnerable. Nobody wants to seem needy. *Everybody is so busy with their own stuff.* To make matters worse, we tend to embrace a myth of rugged individualism: we identify with the lone rider in so many classic Westerns, or the individual achiever. We admire the lone hero. Asking for help seems far from heroic.

Excessive individualism certainly results in sub-optimal performance. Perhaps the greater shame, though, is the lost opportunity to connect with others. Working together builds relationships. How many great friendships have been forged while working on common projects? As one grizzled (or, as he might prefer, "seasoned") project manager observed, "I've turned adversaries into allies just by asking them to help me out. I had to trust them a little first, but then we grew to really trust one another. Someone I once considered almost an enemy is now one of my closest friends, and it started when I absolutely needed her help on a work project. Asking wasn't easy; it kind of sucked, but it really paid off in the long run."

—⚏—

Conversation Starters:
Take a risk that pays off: reach out to others and ask for help. Chances are, you'll do better work, and have fewer strangers in your life. You will also help others to contribute and to connect in meaningful ways. What could be more heroic?

- What keeps you from asking for help?
- What can organizational or team leaders do to create an environment more conducive to seeking assistance?
- Describe an instance where true teamwork achieved something special.

More about Bullying

September 2007

This journey begins with a radio show I chanced upon, in which storyteller Amy Salloway was describing her experience of being bullied for being fat, as a child and as an adult.[26] The story touched me, and led me to think about the connection between bullying and principled leadership. I have since read more of her work, and find it to be smartly funny – that is, her truths are funny, and they often smart a little. Salloway understands bullying, and many other aspects of the human condition.

Bullying involves hurting, scaring, or intimidating someone who is not readily able to defend him- or herself. It can entail physical harm, verbal or non-verbal threats or intimidation, or some combination of behaviors.[27]

Indeed, there is a growing body of literature on bullying, part of a widespread campaign to stop childhood bullying. Among the apparent drivers for this campaign are the very public, very violent acts perpetrated by victims of bullying seeking revenge, either direct or indirect. Beyond remembering tragedies like the killings at Columbine

---

[26] The radio program was *In the Loop*, a program last broadcast in 2010. Learn more about Amy Salloway at www.amysalloway.com or www.facebook.com/awkwardmomentonstage. She is a remarkable storyteller, writer, and performer.

[27] As this book is being published, bullying remains a hot topic, and many resources are available. I found a good description, along with some other interesting resources, at http://stopbullyingnow.hrsa.gov/index.asp.

High School, we resonate with an effort to stop bullying because we have all been exposed to it, either as perpetrators, as victims or as bystanders. Truth to tell, most of us have probably acted in each of those roles at one time or another. I've already apologized to my younger brother, for example.

Echoes of the Past

The topic hits close to home for me, and not just as a wildly imperfect older brother. I was picked on a lot in grade school – I was fat, slow of foot, and loud of mouth. I also had the kind of vocabulary that got kids picked on, and literally no instinct for fighting. Those social experiences hurt a lot, and they were certainly formative.

A couple of years ago, just after our mother died, my brother and I undertook the sad process of dismantling our childhood home. Mom saved stuff. Lots of stuff. In drawers, in boxes, on shelves. In the course of sorting through it all, I found a letter written to my parents by my first summer camp counselor.

As a 10-year-old, my experience at the camp had not been pleasant. My cabin was essentially led by two bullies, who immediately identified me as an easy target for ridicule and observed that none of the other kids would stand up to them. I remember a few of the boys liking it, actively participating in the jeering and pranks, and a larger number looking frightened, neither participating nor objecting. Their primary fear was that they were next.

I had not thought about the experience in many years, until I found the counselor's letter. The first part was mimeographed (it was produced before photocopiers were widely available). The document described a wonderful camp experience shared by all the boys. Then the counselor added a handwritten note of about equal length, stating in essence that "Chad had trouble fitting into the cabin," and advising my parents to help me "learn to act more like a kid," so the other kids would like me more, or at least would pick on me less.

Reading these words as an adult enraged me. Some of my rage was undoubtedly an echo of the distant past. I think that more of it was contemporary, as I read the paragraphs blaming a 10-year-old boy for inviting bullying by being different from the other kids. That was terrible advice, and it represented the counselor's unfortunate failure to teach the entire cabin – the bullies, the victims, and the bystanders – some truly valuable lessons.

As I reflected on the letter, though, my rage faded. I remembered the counselor as a jock and a freshman at a local bible college, probably about 19 years old. He was trying to make sense of a situation based on his experience and from his perspective. As a 10-year-old, he was probably among the cowed bystanders. His advice to me was simple: appease the bullies and avoid their predatory gaze, which could move me from victim to bystander. That was the best advice he had.

Progress

I mentioned the emerging literature on bullying, and the concerted efforts to stop it among children.[28] My own young children are each in educational settings that actively seek to diminish bullying. The results have been mixed, but I've seen excellent examples of progress. The adults become actively involved, in a few ways. They definitely intervene to stop bullying behaviors. More important, they create environments and enforce standards that do not tolerate bullying. Perhaps most important, teachers actively empower kids to stop bullying when they see it, and to resolve disputes effectively and non-violently.

Frankly, when I first heard of these efforts, I was skeptical about whether adults really can influence playground life very much. I subscribed to the *Peanuts* view of childhood, wherein kids hear the words of adults as a vague buzzing sound. As I observe the interventions in action, however, I believe that they can be effective.

The key seems to be empowering the bystanders to actively stop, and thereby prevent, bullying. Many schools have programs that foster

---

[28] When I wrote this piece in 2007, the literature was emerging; in the intervening years it has burgeoned, along with awareness of bullying in schools, workplaces, online...wherever human beings interact. I applaud these efforts, and hope for their sustained success. Based on the experience of my kids and their friends, it seems that school cultures continue to change for the better. I'm not entirely confident that the same can be said for workplaces.

and reinforce the skill and the will in kids, teaching them how to be intolerant of bullying. Thirty-odd years ago, a camp counselor advised me to fit in so I wouldn't be the victim. Today, teachers empower my kids not to let bullies get away with it. That's progress, and it is inspiring.

Implications for Grown-ups

Many kids today are learning an early, practical lesson in ethical leadership. They are being taught that it is their responsibility to stop bullying using non-violent means at their disposal. They are learning to use their personal power to influence others to do good, and that the solution to aggression begins with themselves.

Amy Salloway was right in observing that bullying doesn't stop in grade school. It is rampant in the workplace, as well. Sometimes it is just as overt as it was on the playground, but often it is more subtle, more insidious, and as such, more destructive to our organizations.

I once observed some subtle bullying while facilitating a client's workshop on product innovation. We had convened a panel of outside experts to share their perspectives with a room of participants ranging from interns to senior executives. As planned, members of the audience raised questions, and the panel addressed them. Then I heard the senior executive in the room snicker at some of the questions, first *sotto voce* and then quite overtly. Then he began to dominate the discussion, both by virtue of his own questions, and because none of his subordinates dared to utter a word until his cell phone rang and he left the room.

I approached him at the break, led him to a private alcove, and shared my concern that his behavior was inhibiting others from contributing. "I don't care if they contribute," he retorted, with anger rising. "I care about squeezing as much information out of these panelists as possible, and their questions weren't helping." When I observed that the questions were coming from the very people who needed the information to develop new products, he countered with his view that "the junior people don't know what they need to know," adding that, in any case, he "doesn't have time for people who are afraid to speak up." I tried to respond, but he waved a hand in my face, turned around, and left.

I stood alone in an alcove. My chest was tight, my jaw clenched in anger. I had no investment in this situation beyond my involvement that day, but I couldn't seem to advise my nervous system of that reality. I forced myself to breathe slowly and relaxed my fists, then my shoulders, then my jaw. I returned to the session, only to learn that the executive had been called away from the rest of the meeting. The discussion went beautifully from that point on.

I later heard that *fearless leader* frequently berates people in public. In fact, his performance that day had been entirely subtle by local standards. He also bears grudges against those who challenge him. I wondered about his ascent to his current role, and questioned the future of his organization.

In the two weeks following the meeting, I received unsolicited resumes from three people in the room, inviting me to circulate them to other clients who might be seeking their talents. (That has never happened before or since.) Two came from stellar performers, each with more than 15 years tenure. I called one of them and inquired. He wasn't leaving because his boss was a bully and a jerk. He was leaving because the company continued to promote bullies and jerks, and he figured that it didn't bode well for him or for the organization.

Bullying Costs

Bullying costs organizations directly and indirectly. Years ago I did a different research project for another firm, wondering about the commercial viability of a product line expansion. It quickly became clear to everyone except a single executive that this new offering was a very, very bad idea. In my interview with that executive, she said, "If you want your relationship with our company to continue, you will conclude that this project is highly viable." Unfortunately, it simply wasn't. I told her we had to be objective, expressed our concerns about the project, and offered only to keep her apprised of our progress. We

Charles A. Weinstein Ph.D.

recommended against the project, which was ultimately killed. We continued to work for the company.

Our consulting fees for that research project were nothing more or less than the partial cost of bullying in that organization. Every reasonable person in that firm knew the answer before they engaged us. Bringing in an outsider was the only way for subordinates to kill a bad project while remaining employed. What other costs do organizations bear?

Just One More Story

Years ago I worked for a small company that brought in a new VP of sales. As sales performance continued to disappoint, Mr. Sales decided that the best defense was a good offense. It turned out that being offensive was among his greatest gifts. In management meetings and in his office, he leveled scathing criticisms of everyone around him, illustrating his diatribes with spurious whiteboard graphs. He continued the tirades via email, backstabbing and front-stabbing and side-stabbing – you get the picture.

When people brought their concerns to the CEO, he assured us that he was aware of the issue, and that he was working on it. Further, he argued, Mr. Sales needed the time to succeed or fail on his own merits. That was actually an admirable approach, so long as the CEO was also engaged in correcting the behavior itself. I believe that he was.

After Mr. Sales visited a Fortune 100 company, our CEO received a phone call from a senior executive of that firm: "Tell that [expletive deleted] that the good news is, I have his notebook, and the bad news is, I read it."

Mr. Sales was presenting a major proposal, and had listed the names of people around the table. He then jotted down mnemonics like "Fats," "Idiot," and worse beside many of the names. The prospective client made it clear that we were no longer being considered as a vendor. (I could not help but wonder what was jotted by his name.)

This came as no shock. People who exhibit intramural bad behavior aren't just a risk to internal harmony. They are equally likely to damage relationships with clients, vendors, shareholders, and others.

What's Next?

Leadership is so much more than direction, so much more than influencing others. Leaders have the power to create and foster organizations where bullying isn't tolerated, and where effective collaboration and support for colleagues and subordinates is rewarded.

—⟋⟍—

<u>Conversation Starters</u>

Workplace bullying hurts people and harms organizations. We all have a responsibility to stop it when we can.

- Are you prepared to confront a bully? What factors would encourage you to do so? What factors would discourage you?
- What would it take to rehabilitate the bully, or to help that bully to change?
- If you see bullying in an organization, what does it say about that organization? What would it take to fix what is broken?

Sandlot Mentorships

August 2011

A mong our client organizations, mentorship programs are sprouting like sunflowers. This idea isn't new, but it seems that this year has brought a steady increase in inquiries from senior leaders – from sheriffs to nursing home administrators – about the best ways to promote mentorship in their organizations. Typically, these leaders first think in terms of organized programs, assigning mentors and protégés and setting expectations for their interactions. Many have recently launched programs designed to promote mentorship in one way or another.

The reasons behind these programs are sound. We want to build networks of strong working relationships. We want junior workers to benefit from others' experience, and senior workers to benefit from sharing that experience. We may want to bridge generational or cultural divides. So, we establish programs that push people together and encourage them to...do any number of things. These programs can yield great benefits for participants, and for organizations and broader communities. Good things happen. At the same time, leaders would do well to look for additional, more organic ways to bring about those benefits.

The idea of mentorship is surely as old as humanity. The term itself recalls Mentor, a character in Homer's *Odyssey*. Mentor is a manifestation of Athena, Goddess of Wisdom, who guides Telemachus, the hero Odysseus's son as a young adult. Historians and linguists estimate that the Odyssey was first written in the eighth century BCE, and was shared orally long before that.

To this day, we see mentors as guides and teachers, and sometimes as surrogate parents. Many people reserve the title of mentor for deep and enduring relationships; for others, a mentor might just be someone who teaches us something as he or she passes through our lives. There's no right or wrong answer here, but it is very important that mentors and protégés have reasonably common expectations. That's true for any significant relationship.

It's not surprising, in organizations with employees and contractors passing through, that leaders would want to create structures to promote teaching and professional development. If people don't connect on their own, or if a manager doesn't know whether her people are connecting, perhaps a program to push those connections can help. Still, there's a bit of tension between the ancient idea of one person naturally guiding another and the very modern idea of a management program requiring people to do so. And, to put this sense of tension in perspective, it is worth noting that Homer's Mentor was paired with young Telemachus through divine intervention.

I grew up in the first generation of organized-recreation kids. We generally played our sports in park leagues, Bantam Leagues, Little Leagues...even school recess featured an adult-supervised kickball game. My late father waxed nostalgic (with annoying frequency) about the relative merits of sandlot sports: kid-generated street hockey, basketball, stickball, or whatever. Clearly, there are tradeoffs. Adult supervision probably leads to faster, more even skill development and fewer black eyes, while kids learn different lessons by having their own fun (at the cost of some black eyes).

The same might be said of mentorships. As workplace interactions become less frequent and more intermediated (as in, *"pls txt me tht"*), a bit of prompting and structure may grease the skids, promoting relationships which might not otherwise develop. By the same token, I would hate to think of mentorship only in terms of structured programs or high-overhead relationships. Life leaves plenty of room for pick-up games: casual offers of assistance, and connections and relationships that develop naturally.

Mentorship programs all have the same intent, and we can learn from it. Connect, in person as well as online. Get to know someone newer or older, do some work together, go for coffee or happy hour. Then, participate in whatever programs make sense, too.

—ɯ—

Conversation Starters

Being a mentor or protégée is precious. Let us make room for mentorship, formal or informal, in our lives and in our workplaces.

- Who are your mentors? What do you hope to learn from them?
- Who are your protégés? What do you hope to offer them?
- What are the essential features of a meaningful mentorship?
- What can you do to encourage mentorship relationships among your teammates, or in your organization? Do you need a structured program? How can you achieve those benefits more organically?

Virtue Friendship

"As iron sharpens iron, so one person sharpens another."
– Proverbs 27:17

December 2013

One implicit goal of Ethical Leaders in Action's leadership programs is to encourage participants to forge relationships that help them grow as leaders. Sometimes those relationships take the form of classic mentorships described above. A more experienced mentor shares wisdom and offers guidance to a less experienced protégée. These relationships have immeasurable value. By the same token, sometimes we can learn just as much from our peers. This is especially true when peers become friends who care enough about one another to expect, and celebrate, our best nature.

As Solomon's Proverb would suggest, this isn't a new idea. Aristotle called these relationships, "virtue friendships," or "friendships based on what is good." These are the friends we can count on to call us on our shortcomings, to reinforce our strengths and to take genuine pleasure in our successes. Such relationships are rarely casual, and tend to be enduring and significant in our lives. They represent an investment, perhaps some level of personal risk, and the potential for enduring benefit.

Successful professionals tend to have these people in their lives. I know cops, lawyers, nurses, fire chiefs, and accountants who attribute their successes and achievements, in part, to former classmates, teammates, and others with whom they have connected along the way. Sometimes a mentor becomes a virtue friend as the protégée develops. Other times, friendships are forged by the shared challenge of a tough assignment or a new promotion. However they are formed, these relationships tend to endure.

Why aren't these kinds of friendships more prevalent in our workplaces? Sometimes we are forced (or inclined) to compete with one another for opportunities or rewards. Too frequently, we are so pressed to meet our own individual or team goals that we aren't always willing to help others, or to seek help beyond our most immediate needs. Our teams and assignments shift so often that we don't really get to know our teammates. At times, we forget that connecting with others can be fun – or we don't feel like we have the time or energy for that kind of fun. That's a shame.

None of these barriers is insurmountable, if we recognize the value of connecting, and reach out to others. Fire chiefs in particular seem adept at building these virtue friendships with other chiefs. They rely on these friends to help them make decisions, to reflect and learn from experience, and to mitigate the natural loneliness at the top of an agency. They share a lot of laughs along the way. While the underlying commitment and benefits are serious, the process doesn't have to be, at least not often.

The rest of us can learn from these leaders by cultivating virtue friendships. Look for opportunities to connect, and consciously invest in building these invaluable relationships. Be willing to give and receive feedback, and engage in substantive discussions from time to time. Pick people with whom you like to spend time, too. Enjoy.

—◊—

Conversation Starters

Virtue friends are truly invested in one another's development as people.

- Who are your virtue friends? Does this essay describe those relationships?
- What other types of friendships are important in your life and work, and how would you characterize them?
- What are the hardest aspects of being that kind of person for someone else? What aspects are most rewarding?

Vision That Matters

January 2012

I am currently helping the senior leaders of an organization craft a vision that will guide them over the next five years. As I worked with one team, the team leader voiced a very common, and valid, concern.

"Wait a minute," he said, "we're all busy. Why should we be wasting time and money on this?" He went on to share his view of vision statements: "Very expensive random words, framed on a conference room wall, and never thought of again." He likened our intended outcome to a substance that might politely be described as bovine-derived fertilizer.

I had to concede that I've seen many such statements, and I've worked in organizations (and conference rooms) that sport them. Many were crafted by consultants; every single one began with abundant good intentions. So, how can we make a leadership vision – the content, more than the statements themselves – a valuable, strategic leadership tool instead of so much framed wallpaper?

A vision is a description of the future that can guide and motivate people to bring it about. It is a product of practical, applied imagination. Having a goal and a plan for pursuing that goal is important. Even in tactical contexts, we are either working our plan, or reacting to others who are working theirs. At a strategic level, a clear and meaningful vision enables us to organize our efforts, to evaluate our progress. On an even broader, more personal level, clear vision can help us find meaning in our lives and prioritize how we spend our time and treasure.

It may be helpful to look at a leader's vision from the perspective of a follower. I have worked for leaders who discounted vision, who simply responded to whatever came their way. It always felt like we were playing defense and rarely, if ever, felt like we were truly making progress toward anything. The days and weeks passed, sometimes slowly and sometimes quickly. I looked back and wondered whether I had gained years of experience, or whether I had just experienced the same year, over and over.

I've also worked with leaders who saw themselves as highly visionary. They had many ideas about where we should be heading, and how we should get there. You may have had this experience as well: you take a phone call at 10 p.m. and get urgent instructions, which you hasten to execute the next morning. By noon, you bring the results to your supervisor, who has forgotten all about the last great idea, and is on to the next. An effective leader crafts and applies vision by blending responsiveness with steadiness.

Dream On – and then Think Hard

Effective vision also blends imagination with analysis. We need fresh imagination to pick goals and destinations that help us achieve our fullest potential. We also need hard, clear thought about whether our dreams reflect the right goals, and how we can best achieve them. Toward this end, I have led groups to create a shared vision by moving from creativity into analysis.

We begin by stimulating creative thought about what could be; I like to call it "dreaming," unless the team objects too strongly to that term (plenty of teams lack any sense of mirth). "Ideation" is a trendier term. Team members can dream (ideate?) alone or together, and they are asked to record the product of their imagination, even if that product is highly vague or highly improbable. Participants then evaluate their ideas in terms of four factors, described below. Some dreams become more specific and clear as a result of that evaluation, and others are dropped. Even for those that don't "make the cut," I ask participants to note what they learned from those dreams.

Group members then come together to collect, compare, and often combine the ideas that came out of evaluating their dreams. They do another round of analysis, using the same four factors, and narrow and refine their concepts into the facets of an organizational vision. Sometimes this process goes farther into strategic planning, developing strategic objectives based on the organizational vision, and initiatives to achieve the objectives. It need not go so far to be valuable. Simply defining what we want to be, and how we want to become (or continue being) that together, can be extremely useful.

The process I described is art, not science. Specifically, the art is in stimulating everyone to think both creatively and analytically. We give people the freedom to dream, in part because they are assured that all ideas will be seriously considered. We give even dreamers a straightforward framework for analysis, based on four simple factors:

- **Impact:** Why does this vision matter? What are the expected benefits? What are the negative consequences of any changes, and how might we mitigate them?
- **Reach:** What is the "distance" between our current reality and our future vision? Is our vision readily attainable, or will it require high levels of effort, resources, or risk? How long might it take to see progress, or to come to fruition?
- **Scope:** Who and what are involved in the realization of this vision? Who must take action, who might be involved and whom will it affect? The scope of a vision could be as narrow as a single individual, or as broad as the universe.
- **Clarity:** Have we thought through specifics? Can we articulate our vision in ways that engage others in helping to bring it about?

Any powerful vision is a shared vision, created by a team and valued by team members. Leaders play a particular role of igniting a common interest in creating or preserving something of value, and stoking the ongoing commitment to bring it about. Leaders in all roles become the stewards of their groups' visions, working to empower others to make them real. That ongoing job is easier if the vision itself reflects some up-front work and some refinement from time to time, as well.

With due attention to the quality of our vision, we stand a very good chance of pleasantly surprising – and ultimately engaging – even the staunchest skeptics. We have the framework for planning and executing our work together, and for celebrating our successes.

—⁊⁊⁊—

Conversation Starters

Vision is a clear, action-oriented picture of where we are heading and why. Teams and organizations benefit from a shared vision, and from the process of creating that vision together.

- Do you have a vision for yourself? For your team and organization? How was it developed?
- Do you believe that members of your team or organization have a shared vision of what you are trying to achieve together?
- Can you take the time to dream, and then consider those dreams?

The Cost of Poor Leadership

May 2009

I had a most interesting conversation with some close friends about their childcare experience. Their infant son has been attending a center run by one of the national firms. This company's fees are relatively high, approaching twice the market rate for home-based child care. Our friends were happy to pay that rate, both for the center's explicit brand promise of an excellent, developmentally-oriented experience, and for the assurance of standards, processes, and the resources to execute them. However, they will soon be leaving that center, after just a few months.

It wasn't a disaster that led these parents to look elsewhere; it was an accumulation of smaller disappointments. The teachers gossiped about other infants and their families. The parents were irked when their child was introduced to some highly processed foods at lunchtime, against their prior instructions. One afternoon the head teacher told them (in the tone of a humorous anecdote rather than a contrite apology) that their child had been eating scraps from the floor beneath other children's high chairs, "because he just kept going over there." The care was not excellent. Standards were not upheld.

The parents began observing more closely. They noted that the student/teacher ratio fell below state standards, for more than just a few minutes, more than just a few times. They met with the director, who seemed neither surprised nor concerned. It was time to go.

The center in question is fully accredited and touts its high rating in an impressive array of marketing materials. Its Parents' Handbook discusses a developmental curriculum and details the many ways that teachers communicate with parents. "It was like they were describing a different center altogether," scoffed our friend, the mom, on her way out the door. She acknowledged that staff members were basically friendly, and clearly cared about kids. They had the resources they needed. What went wrong?

Our further conversation revealed the critical theme: nobody at the center was motivated to do more than what was required. The result was mediocrity, at best. Teachers who came in excited about education and excellent care were taught instead to focus on process compliance. Managers didn't reward – or seem to notice – excellence, and they didn't seek to inspire creativity or commitment to great child care or education. "The manager of my local oil change shop does a far better job of inspiring his people," said the father. "I can see it in the care the technicians take while working on my car."

That's a terrible shame. While enlightened mechanics will tell you that proper lubrication is essential for long engine life, they would also agree that excellent child care is much more important to our collective future than is car care. As a parent, I have known great early childhood educators and great centers, and they make a huge difference for the families they serve.

Child care is demanding work. The pursuit of greatness must be continually fostered, even among talented and committed professionals. Leaders must cultivate and communicate a vision, and be engaged with staff on the realities of execution. Standards must be based on real values, which become a meaningful part of the organization. Employees must be valued, appreciated, and rewarded for achieving high levels of performance. Ethical leadership isn't easy, in that setting or in any other.

The rewards are apparent. So are the results of something less. Even if our friends' former center doesn't seem to care about greatness, the cost of acquiring a new customer far exceeds the cost of maintaining an existing relationship. Economics aside, the greatest cost is the lost opportunity to truly make a difference in the world.

Isn't that always the case?

—∿—

Conversation Starters

Organizational leaders must establish standards and expectations, and then constantly reinforce them. It is not easy, but it is critical for performance.

- Do you have a sense of what great performance looks like in your work? What are the key features? Why does it matter?
- Is your understanding of excellence shared by others in your organization? By senior leadership?
- How does the slide into mediocrity begin? How do you stop it?

The Talk: Doing Better with Performance Reviews

November 2011

As we ease into the last weeks of the year, Americans everywhere will engage in a ritual as predictable as the growing darkness. Across this great land, in organizations of all sorts and sizes, supervisors and employees will sit down to annual performance reviews.

How often do you hear people credit their annual review with providing meaningful insights or prompting real performance improvements? Not nearly often enough, I suspect. And yet, countless hours are spent preparing for and conducting these evaluation processes.

The conceptual intent behind an annual performance review is entirely sound: have a structured conversation to evaluate performance. Recognize achievements and learn from failures; identify key strengths and areas for improvement. Check in. Plan. Somewhere in the execution, however, the process too often fails to meet the expectations of supervisor or subordinate. Nevertheless, each firm or agency marches through its process. By this time, the forms are distributed, the deadlines are set, and the process established. What is a supervisor or employee to do?

Let us do something different this year. Regardless of the forms we use, let us turn performance reviews into creative, constructive, substantive discussions. Let us engage, be candid, and learn from one another.

One thoughtful law enforcement executive will ask each of his team members to commit to one thing that they can do to improve their organization in the coming year. He will also use the meetings to learn more about his people, and to address their questions, comments or concerns.[29]

Feedback must be timely and so an annual review, by definition, doesn't happen often enough to matter. These conversations must take place throughout the year. One fire chief with whom I work carries a small notebook around, recording observations that merit feedback, both positive and corrective. He talks to people while matters are still fresh. Not every comment or direction is welcome, he admits, but each conversation demonstrates that the chief cares about his people, as well as their performance. His annual reviews are simple discussions, focusing on the employees' goals as well as their performance. No five-point scale for him. "Either people meet expectations, or they don't. There's always something to praise and something we need to be working on." He understands the limits of an annual review, noting that "there should be no surprises. My supervisors gotta be talking to their people throughout the year."

Whatever their limitations, annual reviews are an established practice. Since we've scheduled the time and prepared the paperwork, let us make the most of these meetings by engaging in real conversations, and by demonstrating that we care about one another as people, and as teammates. Let us keep those conversations going all year long. Let our performance evaluation processes truly "exceed expectations."

—ᴡᴡ—

Conversation Starters
Make performance evaluation processes meaningful by remaining engaged with team members throughout the year, by focusing on people and a sense of purpose.

---

[29] That leader is Matt Bostrom, Ramsey County (Minnesota) Sheriff, who began this process during his first year in office. He led in the development of the agency's evaluation process, in large part "to assure that everyone has what they need to be successful in their roles, and so that they know that their role is important to the agency and to the public."

- When did a performance evaluation lead you to change your actions? How? What features of that interaction made it especially impactful?
- Name up to three things you would change about the performance evaluation process in which you participate. What impact would those changes have? How can you move to bring them about?
- Who was your most influential supervisor? How did he or she conduct performance reviews?

Courage in the Moment

October 2010

My wife Cathy and I were driving through downtown Minneapolis today, a sunny Sunday afternoon, after celebrating our anniversary. We pulled up beside a taxi cab and then saw a pedestrian, a stocky guy about 50 years old, lashing out at the cabdriver for nosing into the crosswalk. He was enraged, he was loud, and he was vaguely threatening. One especially disturbing part of his invective: "This isn't Somalia, you know!"

I rolled down my window, glared at the guy, and said nothing. He kept ranting as he walked off.

First, I believe that the pedestrian's ranting constituted genuine hate speech, and that it called for a response from someone able to respond. I was able to respond, and chose not to. I didn't want to risk his attacking us in the car, nor did I want to rise from the car, making a fight more likely. It is reasonable and appropriate to balance some duties with risk and reward. On balance, telling him loudly and clearly to stop his racist ranting would have been better than remaining silent. I see my silence as a failure of courage.

I am still somewhat troubled by this event. I know that we cannot change the past; we can, and ought to, learn from it. In that spirit, this moment provides some insight into the challenging nature of courage itself. This instance provides insight into both physical courage, which overcomes a fear of injury, and moral courage, which overcomes fears of embarrassment, material loss, or social isolation.

I frequently remind audiences: rarely can we predict the need for moral courage. This means both that we will indeed face moments of truth, and that we ought to seek moral clarity in advance of such moments. This morning I let one such moment pass, and when my anger at the bigot subsided, I was left feeling disappointed in myself.

In *Profiles in Courage,* John F. Kennedy highlights this self-regard as a key factor in promoting courage.[30] He argues that his subjects, primarily 19th-century senators, risked personal ruin in part to preserve their senses of themselves as principled and courageous. Perhaps I will remember my own sense of disappointment when future moments arise. My calculations will more prominently include the impact of proper action on my sense of self. A little flash of shame is worth it to me, if it helps me to be better in the future.

A broader sense of perspective is in order. Nobody died; harsh words were exchanged. It is also important to consider a momentary lapse along with other acts that more fully represent the person I strive to be. The aim of this exercise is neither self-abuse nor self-denigration, but self-improvement. Let us use the past to prepare for future moments of truth.

The goal, in short, is *encouragement,* in the truest sense of that term.

—⟊—

Conversation Starters

Often the need for courage arises in the moment. We cannot change the past, but we can use it to prepare for future moments.

- Reflect on some moments when you were not your best. What can you learn from them?
- When you don't do what you believe would be right, what holds you back? What do you fear?
- It can be embarrassing to share our shortcomings with others. Who is on your team? With whom can you share those moments, in order to get better?

---

[30] Kennedy wrote the book with (or, perhaps lightly edited the work of) long-time advisor and legendary speechwriter Theodore Chaikin "Ted" Sorensen, 1928-2010. There is more on this text in the next essay.

Encouragement

February 2012

Yesterday marked my second session as a Junior Great Books leader for my daughter and seven of her third-grade classmates. I was nervous. I am not generally nervous about teaching; I groove on it. In this case, though, I knew how fickle these kids can be, I didn't want to embarrass my daughter, and I didn't have any confidence in my ability to predict what might embarrass her. Okay, I'll level with you. I was dry-mouth, shake-kneed scared. I sat in my car in the school parking lot, and contemplated calling in sick.

I never would have predicted that reaction. It took more courage than I would have expected to walk through the door, to meet the class, and to conduct the lesson. Of course it went fine, but it revealed important features of courage. First, as noted in the preceding essay, we don't know when we might need it. Second and more important, we don't know when others are exhibiting it. It may have taken enormous courage for one of your co-workers to speak up in a staff meeting, respond to an angry customer, or apply for a new assignment.

I read John F. Kennedy's *Profiles in Courage* as a high school student; it made absolutely no impression on me. I read it again as an adult, and was quite struck by the accounts that Kennedy and (his uncredited co-author) Ted Sorensen provided of 19th-century senators who risked their careers for their convictions. Kennedy and Sorensen offer remarkable stories of real people facing fears with courage. From them, they discern factors that promote courage:

- Clear vision
- Belief in an organization or institution
- Self-confidence and self-regard
- The moment

We might also realize that we can set about encouraging ourselves and one another by creating organizations that tolerate honest mistakes. I have worked in organizations that were led without vision, and which were unforgiving. People were punished for mistakes, and even for speaking out. Not surprisingly, workers took few risks, and performance suffered in all respects. I have also worked in organizations that were led with vision and driven by meaningful missions, and where people were held accountable but also supported (and, at times, forgiven). Remarkable things happened in those organizations.

This week, I was surprised by what scared me. I suspect I'd be equally surprised to know what scares those around me. In truth, we don't always need to know, so long as we are consistently encouraging and supportive, and focused on what is truly important. There's more than enough courage to go around.

—

Conversation Starters
Courage manifests itself in moments of truth. We can cultivate it over time, individually and especially in relationships with others.
- What secretly scares you?
- Do you see situations where someone is irrationally avoiding something? Do you suppose fear might play a role?

- How can we respectfully, effectively help others to work through the fears that are holding them back? Are we prepared to accept that help from others, and if so, why? What makes it easier for us to accept help from others?

Truth in its Proper Dosage

October 2010

This afternoon I stopped into a new neighborhood deli. The joint seemed abandoned, until the owner came to the counter to take my order. I ordered a sandwich. I waited. I thumbed through a dog-eared *Field and Stream*. I waited some more. I finished the *Field and Stream*, and picked up a month-old *Fortune*.

The owner came back to the counter. "Hey, I'm sorry it's taking so long. The regular cook didn't make it in, and I'm not too good on the grill."

"No problem," I said, trying to conceal my irritation.

"Yeah," he continued. "He's on parole, and when he checked in with his P.O., he found out there was a new warrant. They took him into custody."

Conversationally, where does one go from there? "Um, it's good that you offered the guy a chance," I offered. "I know it can be tough to find jobs."

"He's my brother-in-law."

"Hmm."

He went on to tell me about his efforts to retrieve his cook/offender/brother-in-law's car, and a great deal more about the circumstances that led to his incarceration. Not good. On the other hand, when he is not in custody, the guy is apparently a deep-fry savant and no slouch on the grill, either.

The irony arrived before my meal. The *Fortune* magazine featured an article on the McNeil Consumer Healthcare division of Johnson & Johnson – yes, the makers of Tylenol, formerly corporate heroes for their candid and responsible handling of the first major product tampering crisis. That corporate division is now deservedly under fire, for atrocious quality control and a pattern of denial, deception, and obfuscation.

The article was balanced; the story it told was heartbreaking. A company culture formerly dedicated to serving patients, caregivers and parents – a company culture that redoubled its commitment to excellence and quality following the Tylenol crisis – devolved beyond recognition. The quality team was widely known as "The EZ Pass System," and managers bullied testers to tweak quality test results in order to release questionable batches of children's aspirin. When probably tainted batches of Motrin hit the shelves, the company dispatched teams of contractors to quietly and completely buy up stocks off retail shelves to deflect attention and avoid an official recall.

In prior roles, I have worked as a consultant to a number of J&J divisions. I have seen leaders struggle appropriately with ethical questions and consult their robust ethical framework for guidance. These were good companies. J&J employees actively used their famous Credo to make ethical decisions. I saw them make tough calls that cost real money, because they were committed to doing right.

The article laid out how things changed, and offered some suggestions why. The company was reorganized following the acquisition of Pfizer Consumer Health Care; J&J divisions function autonomously;

managers were under enormous pressure to drive growth and profit-ability. The full story has not yet been told. Regardless of the details, it should be read as a cautionary tale for all of us about the fragility of even an apparently robust ethical culture, and about the need for management at all levels to walk the walk. I hope that this team, or the team that succeeds it, quickly finds the right path and re-learns the importance of maintaining fidelity to ethical principles.

Truth-telling and transparency are good starting points, if not to the level of my host at the deli. He is one business owner who might do better with a little less candor. All in all, though, I feel safer with leaders who err on the side of disclosure.

I am also sad to report that the sandwich was lousy. I'll try again in three to five years, sooner if the cook is paroled for good behavior.

—⚡—

Conversation Starters
Candor is a cornerstone of trust; it is better to be too transparent than to be too opaque.
- In general, we suffer from a lack of candor, not an excess. What truths do we not need to know? What truths might we wish to avoid, even if we ought to face them?
- Have you ever been part of an organizational cultural collapse? What happened, and did it affect the organization's approach to ethics?
- Do you trust some corporations more than others? What is the basis of that trust?

We/They

June 2010

I recently gave the keynote at a local city's annual appreciation banquet for commissioners and board members. The event honored volunteers who assume community leadership positions requiring time, effort, and energy. As I reflected on their work, I realized that perhaps the greatest commitment they make might be summed up as follows: they commit to being "we."

If you are a parks commissioner, *they* didn't cut the parks hours or programs: *we* did it. If you are on a board responsible for streets or sanitation, they didn't raise fees. We did. Indeed, leaders in any role within any organization should regard the "mantle of we" as a significant, if too often-neglected, responsibility.

I have seen the abandonment of "we" most starkly in some of the fire and police organizations with whom I consult. A line supervisor – a fire captain or police patrol sergeant – gives instructions at drill night or roll call that ring out as, "here's another thing *they* are making *us* do...." Who are they? Who are we? Firefighters and cops have no monopoly on this bad habit, and perhaps it seems most stark because of the paramilitary underpinnings of their cultures. Maybe it's just because they actually have drill meetings or roll calls specifically to convey information and direction.

Wherever we sit, being "we" is important, but it isn't always easy. I empathize with line managers struggling with this challenge. When I was a line supervisor, my team members groused about "management." I had to remind them – at times, reluctantly – that *I was management.* Serving in those roles also made me realize that organizational managers have dual responsibilities:

- To participate in and try to influence decision making to the extent allowed by their positions and circumstances, and
- To accept and implement the lawful and moral decisions of the organization as leaders of that organization.

If a manager believes a decision to be unlawful or immoral, she has additional ethical duties. For the vast majority of decisions and actions, front-line supervisors are responsible for understanding what the organization is doing and why, and for communicating appropriate direction consistently, constructively, and unequivocally.

—◊◊—

Conversation Starters

One fundamental responsibility of being a leader is shouldering the *mantle of we,* of accepting some level of ownership in organizational decisions and actions.

- Nobody wants to give directions with which they disagree. If you have had to do so, what did you do to make peace with that position?
- Do you have greater regard for a supervisor who gives direction unequivocally, or for those who express their dissent along with their direction? Why?
- Have you ever been asked to accept and/or implement a decision that you felt was unlawful or immoral? How did you deal with the situation?

Slow Pay: Aligning Actions with Commitments

to Others

December 2010

I teach ethics seminars for accountants in partnership with the Minnesota Society of Certified Public Accountants.[31] Following one such course, a participant wrote concerning the very common practice of companies delaying payments to vendors in order to manage cash flow. In particular, she wondered whether smaller companies should be made to wait for months for payment by much larger client firms.

There are a host of ethical issues here, all stemming from the underlying economics. Late payments benefit the payer (the customer) and cost the payee (the vendor), period. If the vendor agrees to long payment terms, it in essence agrees to be a *de facto* creditor. *No foul.* However, if the actual payment violates the agreed-upon terms, as the question implies, then the slow payer is taking something from the vendor that was not offered.

It's often pretty straightforward. The slow-paying customer has enough power over the vendor that the cost is tolerated. That is often the case with a large customer and a smaller vendor. So, such payers

---

[31] I am grateful to the Minnesota Society of CPAs for years of productive collaboration; we work together to deliver customized training for their member firms and organizations, and I am continuously impressed by their commitment to serving the profession and its members.

choose – consciously or not – to exploit their power over certain vendors in order to manage cash.

There is an argument to be made that this is just how things are done, and that collections are just the vendor's cost of doing business. Slow payment isn't dishonorable, it is merely prudent. That argument isn't entirely unreasonable. But that means that the slow payer should acknowledge its role as a "hardball player" and, perhaps, as an exploiter of a trading partner.

The slow payer might even be playing the role of a bully, discussed in two earlier essays. This may be the case, for example, when the customer calculates which vendors it can kick around, and then sets about doing so, because it can. How much "lunch money" do they collect by paying late? Sometimes quite a lot: companies implement a range of services to speed collection of receivables by even a few days, because time does equal money.

That blade may cut both ways. I consistently argue for the ethical and commercial value of creating stronger relationships. Trading partners who trust one another save money through contracting efficiencies. They create value through collaboration and often through innovation. Playing hardball – or bullying – has the opposite effect. Slow payment, in turn, may lead a vendor to pad its rates or to build in penalties, such as interest fees, to recoup the costs. Vendors may take advantage of any discretion they may have, placing slow-paying customers on allocation or cutting corners when they can. Of course, the customer may not accept (or honor) those terms or accept a degradation in service. In any case, the relationship has become somewhat adversarial. All of these measures and counter-measures represent inefficiencies and avoidable costs, which may exceed the benefit of cash management.

However the economics work out, a slow payer is taking something from a vendor to which it is not entitled. To select victims by virtue of their inability to "fight back" seems especially unsavory. For most large companies, this likely also violates commitments made in their organizational codes of conduct, which often include general language about valuing business relationships and specific language about honoring contracts.

Another phrase is also instructive here: "taking advantage." We use that term to describe taking some advantage to which we are not entitled. Without that connotation, however, we have a basic business practice: seeking and obtaining advantages over other players, to boost our own business performance. One feature of a strategic stakeholder relationship, it would seem, would be at least a tacit agreement not to take advantage of one another, but to seek and share advantages together. In the absence of such an agreement, slow paying seems pretty reasonable. If an agreement exists, either contractual or tacit, then it would seem to be exploitive.

—w—

Conversation Starters

Violating payment terms is a common way that customers fail to honor the vendor relationship. The ethics of this practice depend, in part, on the nature of the agreements and on the relationship between the parties. It is worth considering whether the monetary gain is worth the damage to the relationship.

- Does paying slowly seem like a reasonable business practice, or exploitation? If you reach different conclusions about different circumstances, what factors affect your judgment?
- Is it okay to take advantage of other players in business? Why? What does "taking advantage" mean to you?
- What are the roles and responsibilities of vendors dealing with slow-paying customers, in terms of due diligence and response to slow payment?

I'm Telling Everybody: Fiery Lessons in
Command and Control

June 2009

This weekend I had one of the most engaging – no, make that stunning and breathtaking – experiences of my life. I have tried to weave it into a leadership lesson, but those attempts amounted to a pile of hooey. This essay is mostly "show and tell."[32]

On Saturday I joined the Eden Prairie Fire Department (EFPD) in a live burn exercise, which put me in an actual burning building, doing firefighter-like things in the company of real firefighters and fire officers. It was overwhelming, and nearly indescribable. I was told it would be very dark, very smoky, and exceedingly hot. It was. But for the presence of my teammates, I would have felt like a roasting turkey (albeit a turkey in protective clothing, wearing 15-20 minutes worth of safe air, with access to thousands of gallons of water).

I was amazed by how quickly rooms filled with smoke, and how readily one could become lost or disoriented. I looked at a couple

---

[32] In the years following this event, I have had many more opportunities to participate in training, and to observe fire service, emergency medical service (EMS), and law enforcement professionals in the field. It remains as engaging as these early experiences were, even as I've become accustomed to the techniques and practices. Many agencies have multiple opportunities for community members to learn more about their work, ranging from open houses to "citizens' academies." I strongly recommend them.

of the set fires with an infrared camera and thermometer, and was stunned by the vertical temperature gradients as the fires built, from a few hundred degrees (turkey temperatures) near the floor to more than twice as hot at the ceiling: knock-down, pass-out-whatever-you're-wearing hot. I now understand why kneeling and crawling are important firefighting skills. The training sessions were extremely well run, and intellectually I knew I was safe. That wasn't always how I felt. Mostly, though, it was fascinating to watch how fire behaves in a building, and how fire suppression techniques really work. The hardware was pretty cool, too.

I've had the privilege of working with the officer corps of the EPFD for about a year now, essentially working to develop leadership skills and awareness within the context of a well-run, successful, primarily paid-on-call (what is sometimes called, "volunteer professional") fire department. This is an impressive organization.

In working with public safety leaders, we often discuss the limits of command as a mode of communication. On a training ground, and even more so on a live incident scene, we see the necessity for command. In a time-critical, high-risk situation, command is the best way to achieve coordinated, reliable group action. However, it is also critical to remember that commands work because of common understanding, underlying respect, and trust. A team can respond to a brief, uttered phrase with a complex set of actions *only* if the team has common knowledge and shared expectations. The team members will do so consistently *only* if they trust and respect the commander. They will put themselves in those positions *only* if they trust the command structure and the organization. Perhaps most important, the team will go beyond the commanders' orders to pursue his intent – and provide the needed information back to the commander – *only* if that level of trust and respect has been developed in advance.

It was a pleasure to see command and cooperation in action, and to see a healthy blend of responsiveness, initiative, communication, and enthusiasm across the board.

—⚮—

Conversation Starters

Effective command is necessary in time-, safety- and mission-critical environments. Command integrity relies on shared expectations, trust, and respect that are developed over time, away from critical incidents.

- How do you use command as a mode of leadership? What makes it work – or not work – for you?
- If you are a team member, what kind of command do you respond to wholeheartedly, and why?
- Have you had memorable experiences that helped deepen your understanding of leadership? What were those experiences, and what did you learn from them?

Pay Your Taxes

June 2012

I was confronted with an interesting question last week regarding the ethical status of decisions about paying taxes. In general, following the law is considered to be a basic ethical requirement. Exceptions for unjust laws notwithstanding, we may obey the law to avoid sanctions, but might also be driven by a sense of fairness. If we understand the spirit of the law, we should abide by it as well. So, on that basis, should we pay more taxes than the law requires, if we are able to do so?

I think not.[33]

Going beyond the letter of laws or regulations to honor their spirit is also often cited as an ethical principle. For example, the *Caux Roundtable Principles for Business*, descended from the venerable *Minnesota Principles*, state, in part, that a "responsible business... adheres to the spirit and intent behind the law, as well as the letter of the law, which requires conduct that goes beyond minimum legal

---

[33] This also reminds me of the single most popular joke among my graduate school classmates. "Rene Descartes walks into a bar. The bartender asks whether he'll be dining. He replies, `I think not,' and disappears." As a group, we philosophy grad students were not entitled to count humor among our strengths.

obligations."[34]   In other words, those principles, urge business leaders to go beyond what is required by the letter of the law.

As a principle, doing more than is minimally required by law makes sense in many instances.   For example, we ought to make our workplaces safer than regulations require, and we ought to do less harm to the environment than statutes or regulations allow.   In the context of trust-based business relationships, we don't seek out every loophole or opportunity to gain further advantage relative to our trading partners. We may seek clarity of understanding, but we do so with an eye toward both parties' interests, rather than clinging to a self-serving interpretation of a given contract term.   Each of these examples represents a sound, ethical business practice.

Taxes are different. First, I believe we would be hard-pressed to argue for a coherent "spirit" of the tax code. The code, as applied, results from a mixture of revenue objectives, economic forecasts, and especially policy- and politically-driven incentives. Enforcement is intended to be fair, driven by an accurate application of the code rather than any overarching spirit or ideology.   Our obligation, therefore, is to follow the rules as we can best understand them. This standard promotes a playing field that is as level as the tax code allows, and assures that we are paying "our fair share." In this case, fairness entails compliance with the same code that governs everyone else.

Further, if we choose to make additional contributions to the community, I would argue that there are many more efficient means of doing good with our resources than by paying additional taxes. The private sector is a tremendously powerful engine for social change, good and ill. If generosity might move a business leader to pay more than the tax code requires, then that spirit would be better expressed through gifts to many other agencies, private or public.

---

[34] The *Minnesota Principles* were originally framed in 1992 under the auspices of the Minnesota Center for Corporate Responsibility, now known as the Center for Ethical Business Cultures. Their aim was to provide a normative framework for business leaders to promote accountability and ongoing improvement. The Caux Roundtable, a global organization of business leaders, later integrated the *Minnesota Principles* into its *Caux Roundtable Principles for Business.*

With respect to taxes, we can go ethically wrong in at least two ways. Most obviously, there's a reason that tax evasion (rather than avoidance) is commonly called "cheating." It's wrong. Even if you disagree with the government, or the way it collects or spends revenue, you still have a duty to pay. More interestingly, I argue that it is also an ethical mistake to become obsessed with reducing one's tax burden, at the expense of more productive pursuits. It is true that a dollar saved through legitimate tax avoidance drops right to the bottom line. It is also true that the amount of energy and resources spent to save that dollar might be better allocated to projects that actually grow our businesses or otherwise enrich lives, ours or others. It is both prudent and ethically sound to keep taxes – along with other expenses – in proper perspective.

—⚬⚬—

Conversation Starters
It is often honorable to do more than the law requires. Taxes are a noteworthy exception. Our ethical duty is to pay the taxes that we owe, but no more.

- Do you see following rules as an ethical imperative? Why or why not?
- How much energy do you spend avoiding taxes? Does this effort ever come at the expense of expanding your business or achieving other efficiencies?
- What else might cause you, as a leader, to lose sight of the big picture?

Pool Party Ethics

August 2008

I continue to be inspired by businesses that are succeeding by making wise and creative investments in employees. A friend of mine works for one such organization, a firm that implements technology solutions for voice and data communications – everything from high-end videoconference rooms to private and public network infrastructures. He recently attended a great company party, paid for with "spiffs" from the manufacturers of equipment they install.[35] Spiffs are incentive payments that manufacturers offer to the sales reps of retailers or value-added resellers. This company's sales reps all agreed to pool their spiff payments and use them to sponsor parties for the people who actually deliver the work that they sell. The payments add up to some very serious recreation, at no cost to the company.

This is smart for many reasons. First, spiffs can create at least a potential conflict of interest. A sales rep has an incentive to recommend or specify a product that may not be the optimal choice for that customer. Further, a spiffed recommendation may not be in the best interest of the salesperson's employer, either. The promise of a spiff conflicts – or at least reasonably appears to conflict – with the

---

[35] Thanks to my lifelong friend Neil Posnansky, a charter member of the Ethical Leadership Working Group, for this highly instructive story. It's not the first thing I've learned from Neil about being a good person, but one of many lessons that sticks with me.

free exercise of the salesperson's technical judgment. By pooling the spiffs, this company is eliminating that temptation or distraction.[36]

Second, the sales reps are in a position to collectively reward the people who do the work after the sale is made (and often, plenty of work beforehand, too). A good party is a very tangible "thank you." Building this into the way things are done reinforces how important it is to share each project's pleasures and rewards, along with the work.

Finally, these kinds of social events promote effective relationships across organizational boundaries. It is easier to rely on – and harder to disappoint or ignore – people with whom you have a relationship. Parties offer great opportunities to build and foster relationships. They also create memories and stories to be shared, to the benefit of all involved. Good social events contribute to a constructive, positive work environment. Indeed, it seems that this program does all those things. My friend talked about how people converse at the party who don't have occasion to do so in the course of their work, and how each event seems to bring the teams together.

A little creativity, an interest in doing things right and the willingness to follow through can improve an organization, while someone else picks up the bar tab. Ethics is sweet.

—〽—

Conversation Starters
Invest in employee relationships – and have some fun in the process. Be mindful of the ethical dimensions of employee compensation, as well.

---

[36] In most instances, this conflict is not as ethically troubling as a professional conflict of interest because customers and even sales managers often reasonably expect salespeople to act in their own self-interest. An enlightened salesperson typically sees his or her interest as aligned with the customers' interests, but not always. Very often the salesperson is compensated for making a deal, and is not expected to act primarily as an agent for the customer.

- If you work with incentive pay or variable compensation, how much do these factors actually affect your business decisions?
- Do you expect salespeople to respond to incentives directly, or to act primarily in the interest of customers? What is the basis for your expectations?
- Do your work parties build stronger relationships? What could be done to make them more effective in that regard?

The Bad News, Delivered Badly

September 2008

A close friend was recently laid off, his position eliminated due to a change in strategy and an overall enterprise contraction. He was notified by his supervisor, accompanied by a human resources manager. They presented him with an agreement that was to be signed before he could receive a very modest severance, and then had him escorted off the premises. He was not allowed to return to his office, but was assured that his personal belongings would be sent to him within two weeks.

Years ago, as a junior manager, I was directed to participate in a nearly identical exercise. We were gutting my team, based on a change in organizational strategy. The Human Resources Department led the termination process, which was rigid and swift, designed to minimize the risks of litigation or retaliation. The only humane adjustment I could negotiate was permission for me to return with the laid-off employees – my team members – to help them pack their belongings. I carried some boxes to their cars, and expressed my personal regret at what had transpired, with respect to both our team's prior performance and the termination process.

Just writing about that event nauseates me – not because of the terminations, but because of the way they were executed. Our actions as managers demonstrated clearly that we didn't trust our employees to behave honorably. We revealed a lack of compassion and, more disturbing, a contemptuous mistrust of people who hours before were responsible for critical client relationships, operating decisions, and organizational strategy. We trusted them to run our business with us, until we didn't need them anymore.

When my friend shared his own termination story, his anger was palpable but his response was reasoned. He sought the advice of counsel and negotiated with his former company, turning first to securing the speedier return of his personal belongings. He offered to brief managers on his work in progress, an offer which was rejected. He chose to act in ways that reflected his values and commitments, rather than respond in kind to what he considered a pre-emptive act of hostility.

I understand that this approach to termination is fairly prevalent, and that it is not intended to be hostile. It is intended to manage risks of employee retaliation and to limit legal liability. The unintended consequences, however, include the creation of a potential adversary, and the demonstration to current employees that they, too, are potential adversaries based on events beyond their control. That's foolish.

In fairness, I do not know the likelihood, frequency or even the full nature of detrimental acts committed by terminated employees. Neither do I know the degree to which those acts could have been prevented – or exacerbated – by an essentially rude and adversarial termination process. I just know that treating employees in rude and adversarial ways can't be all good, and it can be quite bad.

I have also seen specific instances where reasonable and respectful transitions led to considerable commercial gains for the employer. By trusting employees to act in ways consistent with their characters, and with the attributes we appreciated during their tenure, we achieved the best possible outcomes under difficult circumstances. We made sales that we otherwise would have lost, and maintained critical client services through personnel transitions. We sought and earned our clients' trust that a new team could continue to deliver, based on the invaluable contributions of the departing team members. None of these outcomes could have been achieved had the employees involved been escorted to the door by security guards.

I am not prepared to call all instances of abrupt termination foolish or stupid – just some of them. We can learn from those examples and consider the full spectrum of outcomes when we determine how to act at this critical juncture in the relationship between a firm and its employees. We can also commit to act as humanely as circumstances allow, even if that entails a reasonable risk. The rewards for taking that risk are both ethical and commercial.

—॥॥—

Conversation Starters

When ending employment relationships, we can choose to act in ways that demonstrate respect for the employees involved. Remaining staff, customers, and others may be watching and learning from our choices.

- In what ways are the interests of an employee facing termination at odds with those of his or her employer? In what ways are their respective interests aligned?
- What principles or guidelines would promote respect for the employee while protecting the interests of the firm? For example, a firm might implement an optional process for structured, supervised transition for workers whenever possible.
- Do you believe that the manner of terminating employment relationships affects morale? Does it affect productivity? In what ways?

Warning: Humans in the Workplace

April 2008

W hen I began studying ethics as it is applied by business, I was introduced to a widely-held belief that business and ethics are inherently separate, and that ethics that govern our lives in general should not be applied to the world of business. I have since heard the same argument applied to non-business workplaces, as well. "There are no ethics beyond our agreement. If it isn't in our contract, we aren't obligated in any way," has been an argument I have heard advanced by both labor and management. It is directly aligned with the notion that a person in business is governed only by the constraints specific to the business and not by what is called, by contrast, "ordinary morality or ethics."

Our work lives are, by definition, a big part of our lives. How, then, can we accept a notion of having one set of moral values for "work" and another for "the rest of our lives?" I believe that we can't.

I recently had dinner with an old family friend, who naturally asked about my work. He made the standard jokes that "business ethics is an oxymoron," and that books on the subject are works of fiction. *Chuckle, chuckle.* Then the conversation turned serious and, upon reflection, moderately disturbing.

My friend began by likening my work to that of the clergy – essentially positing that only the truly faithful (presumably, of any number of faith traditions) would really care about doing the right thing in business. "Business," he said with some passion, "is morally neutral. It's not about right and wrong; it's about profit-making." In the interest of decorum, I said something about the deeply ethical business leaders I've met and changed the subject.

Decorum is overrated. I am still annoyed, days later.

The notion that business and morality are separable isn't new; the noted business ethicist R. Edward Freeman dubbed it "The Separation Thesis" in 1993, and it continues to be a lively topic of academic discussion in the business ethics literature. In general, the separation thesis implies that business decisions are essentially amoral. Some theorists have been arguing against that view, quite persuasively, for years. I'm with them.

We spend much time and energy at work. If we have different moral values at work, or simply suppress our sense of right and wrong there, what does that say about the totality of our lives? Moral values constitute an important component of our identity and are *an essential element of our humanity.* If we are forced – or worse, choose – to suppress who we really are in our work lives, how can we function effectively? How can we feel good about our lives?

It is certainly true that settings and circumstances appropriately influence how we conduct ourselves. Years ago, my elder son began playing rec-league soccer. A few minutes into his first game, he left the field in tears. Thinking he was hurt, the coach sent him over to me on the sideline. Thankfully, he wasn't hurt at all – he was enraged! He had been taught not to push and shove, and that was exactly what the other kids were doing. We had a quick, sideline talk about being aggressive on the field, complete with my pantomime of an attitude of aggression. We also talked about the rules, and about going after the ball and not the other players. He returned to the game with a clearer sense of expectations, and was jubilant at halftime, not for the goal he had scored, but because, "when other kids shoved, I just shoved them back." He remains a gentle person, though somewhat less so on the soccer field.

We are right to act differently in different situations. Our relationships with family members and close friends are different from our relationships with co-workers. Even within the business context, we are right to make distinctions based on our respective relationships (e.g., with supervisors, colleagues, vendors, customers, or competitors), and to act accordingly. At the same time, a coherent sense of right and wrong ought to govern our conduct throughout. If we truly believe that business decisions are amoral and suspend our moral sensibilities in making them, we would do well to remove the mirrors from our washrooms, rather than face our own reflections at work.

That process of adaptation – of acting in ways which are appropriate to circumstances – is perfectly consistent with maintaining a coherent sense of right and wrong across all circumstances. It also speaks to the richness and complexity of a meaningful moral viewpoint. We can be deeply ethical, and still be flexible, within limits, about how we engage the world. If doing my job leaves me with a sense of moral discomfort, it is right for me to examine both my morals and my circumstances. Perhaps I am being a prig, or I am confusing ethics with etiquette. More likely, my pangs of conscience are indicating that I ought to change my actions or lead a change in my environment. This may entail a transformation within a company, or a departure from one. Pangs of conscience can be a powerful force for good in our lives, if we engage in critical inquiry when we perceive them.

Like youth soccer, ethical leadership is a team sport. (Also like youth soccer, it can get messy at times.) Members of effective leadership teams trust one another, to act from motives of organizational success, for example, and to speak with candor about what an organization ought to do and why. If these leaders do not each have coherent moral perspectives, then the processes of reflection – and the resulting organizational improvement – are nearly impossible to achieve.

Great business leaders do not check their morals at the door. They seek opportunities to act in accordance with their moral values, and remain open to learning and growing through experience and engagement with others. Businesses grow stronger by embracing diverse points of view. They also grow stronger by cultivating a coherent set of ethical boundaries and shared values that promote excellence in action. It's only human.

—w—

Conversation Starters

Consistent values and principles should guide us in all aspects of our lives. How we apply them should sometimes be governed by context and circumstances.

- What leaders do you admire who apply ethics consistently in different areas of their lives?
- Do you believe there is any difference between morality in life and morality in business?
- What happens to society when many people see the business world as "amoral"?

Big Finish

E ssays grow from experience, and as the late Gamble Rogers put it, *"Experience is what you get, when you didn't get what you wanted."* [37] The essays in this book reflect a range of thoughts, many of which arose on the road to somewhere else. I hope you've enjoyed each leg of the resulting journey as much as I have.

In my years as a consultant and manager, I have written hundreds of sales proposals. Each was intended to bring a reader – typically, a manager with a budget, a need, and (I always hoped) a sense of humor – to take a next step of engaging me or my firm. One might read these essays as proposals of a very different sort: invitations to see ethics as the positive art of being our best, and to lead by empowering others to improve the world. I propose that we augment our moral sense of duty with a human sense of wonder and a desire to lead a meaningful life in relationship with others. I raise many more questions than I answer, and I wonder more than I am certain. Of a few things, however, I am certain. Among them are these final thoughts:

- Life is too precious to waste. Let us connect with others to make a meaningful difference in the world, and to enjoy life in the process.
- Much of a meaningful life is spent in service to something greater than ourselves.

---

[37] Gamble Rogers was a folk musician and storyteller until his untimely and heroic death in 1991. Listen for yourself at www.gamblerogers.org.

- Acting honorably promotes trust-based relationships and enables us to do great things together.
- We are going to make mistakes. Let us make them with class, by owning them, learning from them, and then forgiving ourselves. Let's forgive others who do so as well.
- There are moral absolutes, but they are neither as rare nor as common as people sometimes imagine.
- Adults should not put ketchup on hot dogs. (This is not a moral absolute, but it is something of which I am certain.)

If you disagree with some or all of the forgoing, all the better. My aim has been to stimulate you to reflect on your own beliefs, and to consider how those beliefs help you to achieve your worthy objectives in life. The next steps are up to you, and they need not be down a single path or in a single direction.

Please connect with me and the Ethical Leaders in Action team in your travels, and to share your thoughts. Visit our Website at www.ethinact.com and drop us a line.

Acknowledgements

This book would not have been possible without the efforts and contributions of many wonderful people. Tom Laughlin, my teammate and friend, shepherded the project from a messy manuscript to a (much less messy) launch. I am likewise grateful to Diane Rose of Rose Communications for her help in framing the book as a whole and for editing and improving the text along the way, and to Jeff Swenson of Swenson Design for his inspired cover design.

I am also grateful to the friends and mentors who read the manuscript and offered insightful comments. Professor Emeritus Douglas Lewis challenged me to sharpen and clarify my ideas and showed me, at many points, how to do so. Nyle Zikmund, John Rogers, Jamie Forman, Bob Karol, Todd Wadsworth, Amy Achter and George Esbensen each provided substantive, helpful advice and criticism that contributed to the quality of work.

The perspective and ideas presented in these essays are also informed by teaching and consulting work done with truly remarkable teammates: Susan Mackay, Christopher Nelson, Mary K. Boyd, Scott Odman, Tricia Schulte, Paul Schnell, Judy Krauss, Dominic Nelson, David Magnani, and John Wolff. Rich Gasaway urged me, repeatedly and in the strongest possible terms, to get this project done. Thank you all.

This work connects me with so many inspiring, ethical leaders, in all walks of life. I am grateful beyond words for the opportunities I am given to learn from them, and to assist as they empower others to improve the world.

Cited Authors and Works

The following authors or works were mentioned in the text, sometimes in passing. We did not want to leave readers without some more specific references. A larger, annotated bibliography of texts on various aspects of ethical leadership follows these brief citations.

1. Bentham, Jeremy, *The Principles of Morals and Legislation.* Prometheus Books, 2008 (originally published in 1789)

2. Cooperrider, D.L., Whitney, D. & Stavros, J.M. *Appreciative Inquiry Handbook (2nd ed.).* Crown Custom Publishing, 2008

3. Covey, Stephen R., *The Seven Habits of Highly Effective People.* Fireside, 1989

4. Freeman, R. Edward, *Stakeholder Management: the State of the Art.* Cambridge University Press, 2010

5. Gladwell, Malcolm, *Blink: The Power Of Thinking Without Thinking.* Little, Brown And Co., 2005

6. Hall, Edward T., *Beyond Culture.* Anchor Books/Random House, 1976

7. Heifetz, Ronald A. and Marty Linsky, *Leadership on the Line: Staying Alive Through the Dangers of Leading*. Harvard Business School Publishing, 2002

8. James, William, *Principles of Psychology*. Cosimo Books, 2007 (originally published in 1890)

9. Railton, Peter, "Alienation, Consequentialism, and the Demands of Morality," *Philosophy and Public Affairs*, Vol. 13, No. 2, 1984

10. Rogers, Carl R., and Richard E. Farson. "Active Listening." In *Communication in Business Today*. Ed. R. G. Newman, M. A. Danziger, and M. Cohen. Washington, D.C.: Heath and Company, 1987 (originally published in 1957)

Bibliography

A s you may have gathered from the essays above, I love books. I often distribute this annotated bibliography of leadership-related texts when I speak, and maintain an updated version on the Ethical Leaders in Action Website, www.ethinact.com.

1. **Abrashoff, D. Michael., *It's Your Ship*.** Captain Abrashoff translates his personal tale of engaging the very challenging crew of the USS Benfold, into practical and substantive guidance for leaders on land (and, presumably, sea and in the air). A striking account of empowering leadership.

    Abrashoff, D. Michael, *It's Your Ship: Management Techniques from the Best Damn Ship in the Navy.* rev. updated, Business Plus, 2012

2. **Beauchamp, Tom, Norman Bowie, and Denis Arnold, *Ethical Theory and Business*.** This is a terribly dense business ethics text, laden with arguments both theoretical and practical. Students object to that density, but admit that the content therein, especially the specific discussions of ethical topics, makes it worth the effort for those who want a comprehensive understanding of business ethics for managers and business leaders

    Beauchamp, Tom, Norman Bowie, and Denis Arnold, *Ethical Theory and Business*. Pearson, 9th ed. 2012

3. **Campbell, Joseph, *The Hero with a Thousand Faces.*** This scholarly account of the hero myth through time and around the world provides insight into how our stories shape our cultures and our consciousness. It is a tough but rewarding read for leaders who wish to harness – and deeply understand – the power of storytelling.

   Campbell, Joseph, *The Hero with a Thousand Faces.* 3rd ed. New World Library, 2008

4. **Collins, Jim, *Good to Great.*** While most people seem to remember the images of "getting the right people on the bus" or the story of the hedgehog, Collins's discussion of "level 5 leaders" is even more compelling and interesting.

   Collins, Jim, *Good to Great: Why Some Companies Make the Leap...and Others Don't.* HarperBusiness, 2001

5. **Crawford, Matthew B., *Shop Class as Soul Craft: an Inquiry into the Value of Work.*** Crawford earned a Ph.D. in political philosophy from the University of Chicago. He was leading a prestigious think-tank, but stopped doing that, and became a motorcycle mechanic instead. This book challenges our social belief that "knowledge work" is different in kind from work that involves our hands as well as our minds. Along the way, Crawford's many sharp and relevant ideas can help us re-cast how we find and make meaning in the work that we do.

   Crawford, Matthew B., *Shop Class as Soul Craft: An Inquiry into the Value of Work.* Penguin Books, 2010

6. **Csikszentmihalyi, Mihaly, *Creativity.*** The author (I won't retype his name here) is known as a key researcher on the phenomenon of "Flow," which we experience when we are truly functioning at our highest levels, smoothly and without cognitive interference. He applies this same approach and perspective to the complex phenomenon of creativity, interviewing

over 100 extremely creative people and offering the rest of us useful observations and concrete advice.

Csikszentmihalyi, Mihaly, *Creativity: Flow and the Psychology of Discovery and Invention*. Harper Perennial, 1997

7. **DePree, Max, *Leadership is an Art*.** Short, sweet, and insightful, this collection of essays amounts to a free-form interpretation of Servant Leadership concepts first outlined by Robert Greenleaf. DePree best contributes to the conversation with specific examples and a rich articulation of his own exceedingly humanistic view of leading an enterprise.

DePree, Max, *Leadership is an Art*. Crown Business, 2004

8. **Gilmartin, Kevin M, *Emotional Survival for Law Enforcement*.** This book has been touted as the emotional equivalent of a bullet-proof vest, and with good reason. Its observations and guidance resonate almost universally with law enforcement professionals, and are relevant for others, as well.

Gilmartin, Kevin M, *Emotional Survival for Law Enforcement: A Guide for Officers and their Families*. E-S Press, 2002

9. **Gladwell, Malcolm, *Blink*.** In this book Gladwell explores the experience of knowing and acting from the gut, detailing the power and limitations of expert, seemingly-instinctive decisions. It offers leaders outstanding insight on when and why we should - and when we ought not - trust our instincts.

Gladwell, Malcolm, *Blink: The Power of Thinking Without Thinking*. Back Bay Books, 2007

10. **Gladwell, Malcolm, *Outliers*.** *Outliers* examines the phenomenon of the exceptional performer, debunking our popular myths about the primacy of individual talent and moxie. It appears that many other factors contribute to exceptional performance, as well. One chapter of particular interest to leaders

concerns airline crashes, and the role of "mitigated commu-nication," when subordinates do not candidly and forcefully express critical views in the face of impending disaster.

Gladwell, Malcolm, *Outliers: The Story of Success*. Back Bay Books, 2011

11. **Goodwin, Doris Kearns, *Team of Rivals: The Political Genius of Abraham Lincoln*.** Many have argued that Lincoln serves as a canvas on which we render the virtues to which we aspire. Goodwin paints a very human, very realistic picture of the man, from which we learn great lessons on the power of emotional intelligence, political judgment, and courage.

Goodwin, Doris Kearns, *Team of Rivals: The Political Genius of Abraham Lincoln*. Simon & Schuster, 2006

12. **Greenleaf, Robert, *Servant Leadership*.** This is the classic, writ-ten by a veteran of the corporate executive ranks, which estab-lished an alternative to transactional, ego-driven leadership. It is a book to be savored and considered multiple times as we develop our own leadership styles and commitments.

Greenleaf, Robert, *Servant Leadership*. Paulist Press, 25th Anniversary Edition, 2002

13. **Harvey, Andrew J. and Raymond D. Foster, *Leadership Texas Hold-em Style*.** The Minnesota Bureau of Criminal Apprehension uses this text in its law enforcement management education courses. It is short on theory and framing, but contains some practical lessons and useful advice for emerging leaders.

Harvey, Andrew J. and Raymond D. Foster, *Leadership Texas Hold-em Style*. BookSurge Publishing, 2007. The website, www.pokerleadership.com, is also an accompanying reference.

14. **Kennedy, John F., *Profiles in Courage*.** JFK's celebrated book tells stories of 19th century senators who risked careers and

relationships for the civic values they held dear. The accessible and compelling text won the 1955 Pulitzer Prize, and deserves our attention for its examples – and discussion – of moral and political courage.

Kennedy, John F., *Profiles in Courage.* Harper Perennial Modern Classics, 2006

15. **Klockars, Carl B.,** ***The Idea of Police.*** This short book looks at the tradition, history, and philosophical foundations of law enforcement. The book shows its age, using the characters of *Hill Street Blues* to illustrate the virtues and pitfalls of professional cops, but Klockars' discussion is as relevant today as it was 25 years ago.

Klockars, Carl B., *The Idea of Police.* SAGE Publications, 1985

16. **Koestenbaum, Peter,** ***Leadership: The Inner Side of Greatness.*** Based in philosophy and the humanities, this work presents a powerful framework for identifying and honing the skills and dispositions of leadership. Koestenbaum's central concept is the Leadership Diamond, with four points – *vision, ethics, courage, and reality* – representing strategies for skills development in support of the central *will to greatness.*

Koestenbaum, Peter, *Leadership, New and Revised: The Inner Side of Greatness, A Philosophy for Leaders.* Jossey-Bass, 2nd ed., 2002

17. **Kouzes, James M. and Barry Z. Posner,** ***The Truth About Leadership.*** These two professors and best-selling authors have collaborated on several highly (and rightly) acclaimed books. *The Truth About Leadership* is a distillation from their other work, providing very clear direction for leaders. A reader need not agree with all of their "truths" to find benefit in this brief, substantive discussion.

Kouzes, James M. and Barry Z. Posner, *The Truth About Leadership.* Jossey-Bass, 2010

18. **Lansing, Alfred, *Endurance: Shackleton's Incredible Voyage to the Antarctic.*** In 1914, Ernest Shackleton led an expedition seeking to traverse the Antarctic continent by dogsled. Their ship, the Endurance, became icebound and was ultimately crushed. Shackleton then led his team of explorers, scientists, technicians, and sailors through an astonishing self-rescue across pack ice and open ocean. Lansing's history, first published in 1959, remains a gripping account of extraordinary leadership and humanity at the extremes of endurance.

     Lansing, Alfred, *Endurance: Shackleton's Incredible Voyage to the Antarctic.* Basic Books, 2nd ed., 1999

19. **Lennick, *Doug and Fred Kiel, Moral Intelligence: Enhancing Business Performance and Leadership Success in Turbulent Times.*** These authors, successful leadership development consultants and coaches, lay out a framework for building on strengths and shoring up weaknesses related to moral reasoning and decision-making. While some of the social science methods underlying this work have been challenged by some of our clients, the overall approach has real value for those who favor a systematic approach to self-improvement.

     Lennick, Doug and Fred Kiel, *Moral Intelligence: Enhancing Business Performance and Leadership Success in Turbulent Times.* Pearson Prentice-Hall, 2011

20. **Leopold, *Aldo, A Sand County Almanac.*** Leopold was a conservationist and scholar who lived and worked in the Sand Counties of Central Wisconsin and at the University of Wisconsin, Madison. This book, published posthumously in 1949, grants the patient reader a remarkable journey. Our contemporary environmental debate is often about what we ought to do or must do. This book inspires us to care about why, and to more fully appreciate the natural world and our place in it.

     Leopold, Aldo, *A Sand County Almanac.* Oxford University Press, 1989

21. **Machiavelli, *Niccolo, The Prince.*** Reading around the historical references and shameless self-promotion, we find wisdom in Machiavelli's timeless advice concerning politics and management – how to obtain and maintain power. It is also worth recalling that Machiavelli holds that the end justifies the means – his most famous quote – only if the end is itself just. In Machiavelli's terms, just ends are those which benefit society.

    Machiavelli, Niccolo, *The Prince.* Simon & Brown, 2012

22. **MacLean,** Norman, ***Young Men and Fire.*** This book contains a compelling account of the Mann Gulch forest fire disaster of 1949, and a somewhat more ponderous story of the author's investigation and reflections on that catastrophe. Fourteen young smoke jumpers were killed when many failures of leadership and execution tragically converged. Strong themes emerge from the narrative, including vision and leadership, and the challenge of leading from vision. This book is especially poignant and relevant for fire service leaders, but has lessons for all.

    MacLean, Norman, *Young Men and Fire.* University of Chicago Press, 2012

23. **Marlantes, Karl E., *What It Is Like to Go to War.*** Marlantes served as a Marine infantry officer in Vietnam. He has also been a Rhodes Scholar, a successful international management consultant, and an acclaimed war novelist. This book is a deeply personal, intellectually rich reflection on his experience as a warrior. It offers especially profound insight for those who face the darker aspects of human nature, in themselves and others.

    Marlantes, Karl E., *What It Is Like to Go to War.* Atlantic Monthly Press, 2011

24. **Minto, Barbara, *The Pyramid Principle, Logic in Writing and Thinking.*** This book is a cult classic among consultants, written

by the first female partner at McKinsey and Company. It earned that reputation by being an absolutely practical, useful primer in how to conceive and communicate business ideas logically and clearly. It is out of print but available used from Amazon and other sources.

Minto, Barbara, *The Pyramid Principle: Logic in Writing and Thinking.* Financial Times Management, 1995. A new revised (2010) edition is available through the Barbara Minto home page, http://www.barbaraminto.com/textbook.html.

25. **Niehardt, John, *Black Elk Speaks.*** In 1932, Niehardt and Ben Black Elk interviewed the latter man's father, Oglala Lakota medicine man and elder Black Elk. The resulting book has been regarded, not without controversy, as a central work of history, anthropology, and theology. Our readers found remarkable insight into ways of encountering the world that are geographically close, and philosophically distant, from our own.

Niehardt, John, *Black Elk Speaks, Being the Life Story of a Holy Man of the Oglala Sioux.* State University of New York Press, 2008. There are also older editions available through Amazon and the University of Nebraska Press.

26. **Perry, Michael, *Population 485.*** This extremely personal essay captures the very personal dimensions of paid, on call firefighting and rescue in a small community. The prose is intimate and striking, touching on themes of life and death well beyond the incident scenes.

Perry, Michael, *Population 485.* Harper Perennial Press, 2007

27. **Philbrick, Nathaniel, *In the Heart of the Sea.*** A powerful, historical account of the sinking of the Whaleship Essex and subsequent travails of her crew, who set out in three open whaleboats to traverse the vast Pacific. The text reveals the pros and cons

of different leadership styles, and especially underscores the ways in which our prejudices can negatively influence our decisions. It is also an extraordinary story, exceedingly well-told.

Philbrick, Nathaniel, *In the Heart of the Sea*. Penguin Books, 2001

28. **Phillips, Donald T., *Lincoln on Leadership*.** This modern classic text is both highly relevant and highly engaging. The author became captivated by Abraham Lincoln as a leader, a human being, and a myth. The book arises from his extensive research, informed by his own experience as a leader. Each chapter addresses a theme, using stories from Lincoln's life to illustrate practical, meaningful leadership lessons.

Phillips, Donald T., *Lincoln on Leadership: Executive Strategies for Tough Times*. Warner Books, 1993

29. **Pink, Daniel, *Drive: the Surprising Truth About What Motivates Us*.** This is a singularly compelling look at human – humane – motivation (and therefore, leadership). Pink faithfully draws upon multiple research studies and perspectives to craft an account of intrinsic motivation, drive that leads to extraordinary performance and meaningful lives. Hint: Except under narrow circumstances, carrots and sticks can do more harm than good.

Pink, Daniel H., *Drive: The Surprising Truth about What Motivates Us*. Riverhead Books, 2011

30. **Salka, John, *First In, Last Out: Leadership Lessons from the New York Fire Department*.** While the insights aren't earth-shattering, Salka's credentials as an FDNY battalion chief and veteran of the 9/11 response and ongoing "overhaul" lend credibility to some solid ideas about strategic and tactical leadership.

Salka, John, *First In, Last Out: Leadership Lessons from the New York Fire Department*. Portfolio Trade, 2005

31. **Senge, Peter M.,** *The Fifth Discipline: The Art and Practice of the Learning Organization.* This classic work presents an approach for building and leading organizations that are highly capable of ongoing improvement, and highly responsive to changes driven by internal and external stimuli. It amounts to an alternative model for management that reflects the knowledge, rather than industrial, age.

Senge, Peter M., *The Fifth Discipline: The Art and Practice of the Learning Organization.* Doubleday, Revised and Updated edition, 2006

32. **Sledge, E.B.,** *With the Old Breed.* A Marine's lucid, candid account of the battles of Peleliu and Okinawa teaches us about courage and resilience in the face of almost unimaginable adversity. Sledge also offers powerful insight into followership, and into the features of command most admired by dedicated followers under the most extreme circumstances. Not for the squeamish.

Sledge, E.B., *With the Old Breed: At Peleliu and Okinawa.* Presidio Press, 2007

33. **Snyder, Steven,** *Leadership and the Art of Struggle.* In this new book (published in 2013), leadership consultant and Microsoft veteran Steven Snyder lays out a rich, comprehensive approach for leaders to consciously grow and thrive through adversity. Snyder presents a wide range of techniques, illustrated by stories from his research, organized in terms of a fairly complex framework. Readers may end up picking some recommendations and discarding others, but they will find useful insights throughout the book.

Snyder, Steven, *Leadership and the Art of Struggle: How Great Leaders Grow through Challenge and Adversity.* Berrett-Koehler Publishers, 2013

34. **Sun Tzu,** *The Art of War.* Master Sun offered a great deal of advice, and leaders can learn most by reflecting on his

observations on the critical nature of preparedness, and the need for ongoing situational awareness. This book is part of the business folk culture, which also raises questions about strengths and weaknesses of the business/war metaphor.

Sun Tzu, *The Art of War.* Oxford University Press, 1972

35. **Sutton, Robert, *The No Asshole Rule.*** The author defines assholes as those who diminish or demean those with less status or power, what we might also think of as bullying. He does a great job of describing bad behavior and its corrosive effects on an organization. He does an even better job encouraging us to curb our own asshole instincts and never to tolerate those behaviors in others.

Sutton, Robert, *The No Asshole Rule: Building a Civilized Workplace and Surviving One That Isn't.* Business Plus, 2010

36. **Tasler, Nick, *Why Quitters Win: Decide to be Excellent.*** Tasler provides a highly readable, compelling argument for being thoughtful and self-aware in our decisions and focused in our actions. His recommendations are relevant, action-oriented, and grounded in sound research.

Tasler, Nick, *Why Quitters Win: Decide to be Excellent.* Motivational Press, 2013

37. **Terkel, Studs, *Working.*** Terkel, a venerable journalist and political radical, interviewed hundreds of people from all walks of life in the nature of and meaning of work. The work consists of excerpts from those interviews and framing essays by the author. By that description, this work may not sound promising, but it is fabulous.

Terkel, Studs, *Working: People Talk About What They Do All Day and How They Feel About What They Do.* The New Press, 2007

38. **Weick, Karl E. and Kathleen M. Sutcliffe, *Managing the Unexpected.*** This book offers remarkable insight and practical guidance on

how to make your organization more resilient: resistant to crisis and capable of recovery from it. It is exceedingly well-researched and equally well-written.

Weick, Karl. E. and Kathleen M. Sutcliffe, *Managing the Unexpected: Assuring High Performance in an Age of Complexity.* Jossey-Bass, 2001

39. **Zimbardo, Philip, *The Lucifer Effect: Understanding How Good People Turn Evil.*** Zimbardo is a psychologist who uses examples ranging from the famous 1971 Stanford (simulated) Prison Experiments to the (all-too-real) abuses of prisoners at Abu Ghraib to illustrate how social factors and other circumstances can "lead good people to engage in evil actions." The book offers a powerful insight, including guidance on how we can reinforce and sustain our moral commitments despite these very real and common dangers.

Zimbardo, Philip, *The Lucifer Effect: Understanding How Good People Turn Evil.* Random House Trade Paperback, 2008

—〰—